my california

my california

journeys by great writers

edited by Donna Wares . introduction by Pico Iyer

ANGEL CITY PRESS

CALIFORNIAAUTHORS.COM
WRITERS.COM

contents

editor's note

Fly-fish the pristine waters of the Lower Owens River. Step up to the microphone in a California honky-tonk. Surf the biggest waves California has ever seen. Mingle with ducks in an urban oasis. Roller skate through L.A.'s Union Station.

My California is the personal journal of twenty-seven of California's finest writers. Their backgrounds and perspectives are as varied as California itself, native and immigrant, longtime and incoming, poets and workaday journalists.

But these writers share a common trait: a generous spirit dedicated to stoking the state's collective imagination for future generations.

All of the contributors to My California graciously donated their work so that proceeds of this book can benefit the California Arts Council, an agency forced to suspend school writing and arts education programs in 2003, and on the brink of extinction because of the state's financial meltdown.

Paddy Calistro, the publisher of Angel City Press, and I both loved the idea of creating a California travel anthology and contributing to the beleaguered Arts Council at the same time. But we wondered: Would others feel the same way?

I mentioned the idea to several writers whose work had been featured at CaliforniaAuthors.com. Instead of hemming and hawing about other commitments, the writers all said yes. No hesitation; no sales job required. Mark Arax, Aimee Liu, Kathi Kamen Goldmark, Patt Morrison, David Kipen and Veronique deTurenne were in. Filmmaker Gail Knight Steinbeck, who often shares dispatches about the sad state of affairs at the California Arts Council, was enthusiastic too, and she quickly enlisted her husband, Thom Steinbeck, to contribute a piece. Kate Cohen, my amazing partner at CaliforniaAuthors.com, offered to donate the graphic design of the book's cover and agreed that CaliforniaAuthors should collaborate on the project with Angel City Press. My sweet husband, Edward Humes, always adept at fending off my outlandish schemes, not only volunteered his own writing, but also rang up novelist T. Jefferson Parker, who eagerly offered an essay too.

Paddy, meanwhile, was getting the same effusive responses. Writers D.J. Waldie and Carolyn See, Angel City Press sales director Chuck Morrell and Scott McAuley, the treasurer and jack-of-all-trades at Angel City Press, jumped onboard. Barbara Whitney at The J. Paul Getty Museum set the wheels in motion for both the museum and the world-renowned artist David Hockney to contribute *Pearblossom Hwy 11-18th April 1986 (Second Version)* for the cover of *My California*. David Hockney offered his incredible photo collage gratis to help the Arts Council. Trish Battistin and Karen Kuhlman in his studio, and Jackie Burns at The Getty all helped make the donation a reality.

Paddy also contacted Malloy Incorporated, the printer for many Angel City Press books, where Bill Ralph and his colleagues generously offered to donate the entire first printing of *My California*. The Malloy team had just one request in return: Please have the book ready for BookExpo America, the publishing industry's annual convention in June 2004. We faced a daunting deadline—it was already December, and both Angel City Press and CaliforniaAuthors.com were deep into work on other projects—but we decided to move forward. We just hoped all the writers would meet our very tight deadline.

And amazingly, they did.

My California came together in divine order. Each day brought more good news: Matt Warshaw was in, then Firoozeh Dumas and Deanne Stillman and Derek Powazak, followed by Rubén Martínez, Dan Weintraub and Anh Do. One morning, devorah major's story unexpectedly arrived in the mail like a surprise birthday present. L.A. book publicist Jackie Green offered help with promotion, and also enlisted novelist Percival Everett, who liked the idea of penning a non-fiction piece to help the Arts Council.

The honor roll kept growing: Gerald Haslam, Chryss Yost and Michael Chabon added their essays, and so did Dana Gioia, the Sonoma County poet who now heads the National Endowment for the Arts in Washington, D.C.

Héctor Tobar, South American correspondent for the *Los Angeles Times*, responded from Buenos Aires in between treks to Montevideo and La Paz. Pico Iyer signed on just two hours after landing in California from Japan. Mary Mackey e-mailed from a Brazilian trip, offering what by now was becoming a surprisingly common refrain: "I am very (very) happy to be able to do something to help counter the horrible budget cuts in the arts."

To each of these extraordinarily talented contributors I offer my heartfelt thanks, appreciation and awe. And I have to add a special thanks for Paddy, who has been tireless in her support of this project and is truly an angel.

I can't think of a better beneficiary for all the generosity fueling *My California* than the California Arts Council. In years past, the Council has provided grants to school-based arts and writing programs, symphonies, ballets, theaters and arts organizations in every corner of the state. The Arts Council's budget has been decimated by a colossal ninety-seven percent since 2000. The situation grew so dire that staff members bought lottery tickets in hopes of keeping the agency afloat.

That's beyond sad. So is the fact that Californians chipped in just three pennies per capita in 2003 to support the arts.

We live in an era when the arts are under siege in our public schools and our local communities—when even the City of Los Angeles came to the brink in 2004 of eliminating its Cultural Affairs Department.

All of us who have worked together on *My California* hope this project will begin a reversal of fortune for the arts in *our* California, raising both money and awareness of the critical need to save the Golden State's creative soul.

—DONNA WARES

introduction

by Pico Iyer

To those of us who came to California from far away—as so many of us do—the place we imagine (and so find) seems located somewhere around the day after tomorrow. Ever since Hernando Cortez named this stretch of land, by some accounts, after a fictional island of the Amazons (fashioned in a fifteenth-century Spanish novel), California, more than anywhere, has been a province of the imagination that confounds most of us who confront it in reality. A state of consciousness, you could say, on which outsiders, who soon become honorary Californians, famously project their hopes and frustrations. It has always seemed apt to me that the home of physical and metaphysical gold rushes—the "Great Western Paradise," as the Chinese called it—is also the place, some say, where the fortune cookie was invented. Fortunes, futures, gimcrack versions of futures: They're all mixed together here, drawing us from afar, potential consumers, potential producers of a dream that—we come to see too late—can best be appreciated from afar.

"It's a state of mind," Robert Redford once said of California's fictional capital, Hollywood, passing on the conventional wisdom, and it's an actual location. The location is scarred, scary and full of those who've lost their way; but as a state of mind, in Redford's words, "it's transporting and unique: the end of the rainbow, the melting pot, the edge of the continent." Or, to put it another way, Hollywood Boulevard has long been a slum, but the Hollywood sign shines in the world's imagination.

This all has become part of the received wisdom of the place, the first cliché for the newcomer to see through; but what the Californian veteran often loses sight of is that the place really has managed to remain one step, one thought, ahead of the rest of us. Perhaps it's only from afar, or only in the eyes of those who have never been to the "broken promise land," that one can see the pattern: a center of the aerospace industry, when people were just beginning to leap across oceans (eight airports around L.A. even today); the epicenter of the Image, just as the whole globe was falling under the spell of TV, the silver screen; then home to the computer industry, the nerve center of the global village; and now ever more a cacophony of discarded futures, longed-for futures, pasts in a state of endless becoming, which seems to speak to the global anarchy of tomorrow.

Yet all of these industries—it's easier to see from afar—are based on teaching the world how to fly. All of California's major exports to the world are attempts to get us to look up from, and beyond, where we are. Outer space is being mapped at Caltech; inner space is being charted at Esalen and the other cathedrals of the "human potential" movement; cyberspace is being pushed forward in Sunnyvale; and California's promise to many of us is that it will eliminate time—erase age, annul the past, leave all sheets clean—by replacing it with space. Infinite horizons.

I write all this as one of the millions who came here in pursuit of all that, drawn by a family from India, living in England, who wanted to put those pasts behind it. The first time I set foot in the state, in 1964, at the age of seven, the little town of Santa Barbara was presented to us as "the Athens of the West." Staring up from a row of eucalyptus trees, the ocean stretching out below—farther than the widest expanses of Oxford, England the skies an exultant blue, everyone around with a light in his eyes, the hope that had brought him here, we could easily believe it.

My father moved us from England to Santa Barbara to join a think tank that was busy creating a new future; the school where I was sent was in an area called Hope Ranch (California has never been shy with its symbols), and Mike Love of the Beach Boys, a character from allegory it could seem then, had a place nearby. Down the coast a few miles was a community founded by spiritualists, given the archetypal California name—Summerland; across the hills was the little town where they'd located Shangri-La for the *Lost Horizon* movie that had given people around the world a new sanctuary to dream of. Up the road, in the years to come, would be Ronald Reagan and Michael Jackson, cocooned in their respective Neverlands.

We didn't stop to think then that we were conflating proper names with high ideals, or that reinventing the weal might involve dissolving even the certainties that had held up humanity for centuries. We knew only that we could find the wisdom of our native India thirty miles to the south, where Krishnamurti addressed the world's innocent in his oak grove; we could revisit Europe, amidst the faux-gingerbread castles and windmills of Solvang, a Danish settlement thirty miles to the north. Somewhere in the middle, conforming to the ideas we'd formed in frigid Oxford, the surfers were drinking wheatgrass juice at the Paradise Cafe and an eccentric old European opera singer was developing a fantastic private garden she called Lotusland.

Exiles, all, living permanently in their heads, we might have seen; people keeping distant hopes alive in a desert that accommodat-ed all. When people stop believing in the conventional deities, as G.K. Chesterton notoriously said, they don't believe in nothing; they believe in everything. And belief is what we came for, the chance to build cas-tles in the air, in a place where the air was big and bright enough to seem to house more constructions than any piece of soil. "Stepping westward," as Wordsworth wrote providentially, "seemed to be a kind of heavenly destiny."

These ideas all seem a little quaint to me now: the Beverly Hills we had eagerly devoured on our TV sets in England is largely speaking Farsi, and Long Beach, where the Queen Mary rests, is the home of the latest L.A. dramas, in which Cambodian gangs face off against Hispanic ones. The passenger disembarking at LAX finds him-self in a swirl of Koreans and Guatemalans and Ethiopians who look nothing like the characters on the soap opera *Santa Barbara* that is broadcast to a hundred nations; the visitor bumping along the streets of San Francisco soon realizes that it does not conform to the *California Dreams* program screened on the government educational channel in Japan. The very arts that have long kept the state afloat, and shining around the world, are ever more threatened, as a California Arts Council budget that was $31 million in 2000 shrank quickly to $26 million and then to $1 million in 2003. (Canadians spend $145 per capita every year to fund their arts, Germans $85 and Californians three cents.) It takes someone from somewhere else—a Reyner Banham, a Christopher Isherwoood, someone who sees the West as "El Norte" or Taiwan East—to look past the two thousand street gangs, twenty thousand sweatshops and one hundred thousand home-less souls that anti-historians of L.A. grimly enumerate.

And I, after forty years here, see that endless summer has its problems, if it refuses to take in winter and fall. The street that leads to the beach volleyballers' paradise in Santa Barbara is called *Salsipuedes* and, trained now in Spanish by California, I can see that this means, "Leave if you can." Perpetual youth can be a kind of sadness, and endless reinvention sometimes feels like the Hollywood script of legend, the self in permanent development and being worked over by other hands. But reality—what remains when the projector stops rolling—was never what brought us here, and it will never be reality that causes us to stay. The gift of California, for those who have not just dreamed of it, but dared to stake everything on those dreams, is to look far beyond the everyday, and in the general direction of the stars. It was just when Nietzsche pronounced the death of God, we tell ourselves, a little hopefully, that California, our California, was first conceived.

Pico Iyer has been writing about his adopted home on and off for twenty-five years now. He is the author of numerous books about the dance between cultures, including *Video Night in Kathmandu*, *The Lady and the Monk*, *The Global Soul* and *Abandon*, an Islamic Californian romance. His latest book is *Sun after Dark* (2004).

Iyer's work often appears in *Harper's*, *Time* and the *New York Review of Books*. He divides his time between Japan and California.

the big valley

by Mark Arax

I live in an old fig orchard in northwest Fresno just off Forkner Avenue, a street named after the King of Figs. My younger sister and brother live a mile or two down the road, and each of our houses sits within walking distance of where we grew up. When my father claimed our first piece of fig ground in 1968 and built a custom house with a swimming pool out back, it was easy to believe we were living on the far fringe of existence. I rode my minibike through the figs that wrapped around our house and gigged for frogs in an irrigation canal that sliced through the neighbor's backyard. With one orchard stitched to the next, it was easy to lose your sense of geography and time.

One afternoon I ventured too far and got lost. It couldn't have been more than three or four miles, but it seemed as if I had found another world. The engine of my Li'l Indian had overheated and I was stuck in the mud, surrounded by hundreds of turkey vultures. They were the ugliest things I had ever seen, heads naked and wrinkled and forenecks the color of blood. They looked hungry and determined, not the sort of the beast I could frighten off with a dirt clod or a shout. I imagined all sorts of cruel ends. Luckily, my cousin Brian had been riding beside me on his motorbike and steered clear of the mud. Under the long eye of the buzzards, we hitched my bike to his and putt-putted home, taking in what remained of the fig empire that J.C. Forkner had built in the early 1900s.

My grandfather arrived here when Forkner was still blast-ing two hundred fifty thousand holes in the hardpan to plant his Calimyrna figs, a cross between the California and Smyrna varieties, new world and the old. "Boom, boom, that's all I heard," Grandpa told me. "Dynamite day and night. The whole Fresno, it was shak-ing." Henry Ford himself had come out to Forkner's Fig Gardens to watch his new tractors dig twenty-five miles of canals and level twelve thousand acres of hog wallow. Never had so many Fordsons been assembled to work one piece of ground, our local history books crowed.

Grandpa was a survivor of the Armenian Genocide, a young poet who took his pen name from the River Arax that came down from Mount Ararat, and he did what all young poets do when they find this new land. He fell to his knees and began picking. It took him four seasons tramping up and down the San Joaquin Valley to buy his first vineyard. My father grew up on the farm, left in 1950 to pursue a football scholarship at USC, and then came back. By the time I was growing up, he ran a grocery store and then a bar. The only vineyard I knew was the one in a painting that hung above our adobe fireplace. Right next to the frame was a stain from a stick of butter he threw at me in a fit of rage. My dad wasn't an easy man to figure. In the draw-er, he kept a knife that looked different than every other knife and when I asked him what it was for, he simply said, "girdling grapes."

Why he kept it there, what girdling even meant, were questions that didn't occur to me for another twenty years.

By the time I learned that the curved double blade was used to cut gashes in the vines' outer wall, scars that kept nutrients from flowing down into the trunk where they were wasted, our world had changed. Men sharing my father's vision had bought up parcels all the way to the river. Today, the fig orchards of northwest Fresno are gone, swallowed up by custom houses and tract houses, Wal-Marts and Targets, and so many fast-food chains that when McDonald's wants to launch a new product nationwide, it does its first tests here. People now talk about my part of Fresno as if it were the inner city. The transformation happened in half a lifetime. "Joe-Joe," I tell my oldest boy, "I remember when all this was . . . " And then I catch myself, an old-timer at forty-something. "Let's go take some batting practice."

The roots beneath the clay die hard. In early spring, they send up shoots through the crannies of my backyard. Up from the ivy and bamboo come Forkner's old figs. I attack them with shovel and shear, out of suburban necessity, I imagine, but the milk they bleed, sticky white, causes me to wonder. And yet my deathblow is something of a paradox, for I have turned large sections of flowerbed and lawn into orchard and vegetable garden. Like my grandfather and father, I am a backyard farmer with too little land for my dreams.

Enough dirt remains under my nails that I sometimes buttonhole real farmers with tales of how my fifteen varieties of tomatoes keep producing through early December (I forgo commercial fertilizers that cause the plant to leap out of spring and produce too many watery tomatoes too fast, only to peter out come summer. I use compost and rabbit droppings instead.) Or how my peppers do better in slightly heavier ground and my cucumbers in slightly lighter soil, requiring the creation of mini zones in a plot no bigger than fifteen yards by ten yards. Of course, the real farmer shoots back a smile that tells me I can't begin to understand how tortured is the logic that compares my backyard to his thousand acres.

Still, I love mixing with the big boys, to hear them whine about too much government intervention and too little government subsidies, about good weather producing surplus yields and low prices and bad weather producing paltry yields and record prices. If I get up early enough, I can find them at the coffee shop comparing the size of their grapes like some boys compare their privates. But if you want the full treatment, to see them in all their beautiful pessimism and optimism, you wait until mid-February and head to Tulare, to the biggest farm equipment show in the world, even bigger than the one in Paris, France.

From Fresno to Tulare is an hour's drive, and I gas up my Volvo and journey south on Highway 99, the flat four-lane that runs straight up the gut of the most productive farm region in the world. Highway 99 has been called our Mississippi, a tidewater of crops and *campesinos*. Every third vehicle that whooshes past the oleanders that divide the road is a big rig and, more often than not, they're hauling away some piece of the valley's lavish bounty. Summer here isn't measured by the calendar but by the pick and pull and squeeze and crush of the unbroken harvest. It begins in April with the cherry and ends in November with the pomegranate. In between we pull more milk from our cows than any other region in the country. The same with grapes, tomatoes, peaches, nectarines, plums, almonds, walnuts, pistachios and olives.

Maybe all kids are dumb to their place, but it hardly occurred to me back then that we lived amid seven million acres of farms from Bakersfield to Redding. Even surrounded by all those figs, we lived a decidedly suburban life. The country might as well have been an ocean away, so few times we touched it. "The country," my mother would chant to my father, as if it were some elixir. "Let's take a drive out in the country." It seemed that we were neither rural nor urban but some fraudulent variant of the two. The bigness of valley agriculture only compounded the distance that separated suburbia from the farm. What we glimpsed on 99 on our way to Disneyland or Candlestick Park wasn't the prettified vineyards of Napa or the gentle wheat fields of the Midwest. The valley had its own rusty, gnarled, corrugated, fermented beauty. Our farmers weren't farmers. They were growers.

Ten minutes outside Fresno, the strip malls and gated communities give way to an open view, and I can make out the faint shoulders of the Sierra. Faint because we now live in the dirtiest air basin in the nation, our eight-hour smog readings worse than even Los Angeles. As I head into Fowler, there's a parting in the oleanders as if some elephant has trampled across, and I grip the wheel tighter. Long stretches of 99 have no concrete or metal barrier separating southbound and northbound traffic. Truck drivers hauling one crop or another are sometimes too drunk or wired on crank to know that they've just crossed the oleander line. The pink flowers part. You never see them coming.

A few miles past Selma, where the "Raisin Capital of the World" has thrown its lot to car dealers, a tractor clears another eighty acres of prime farmland. You can read what kind of year a farmer has had by looking at his fields in late winter. If he hasn't pruned his vines yet, you can bet he's had a tough year. A field cleared like this one sometimes means he can no longer turn a profit, and he's better off sitting on his dirt than growing raisins. If the banks are so inclined, a cleared field might mean he's pulling out grapes and putting in almonds. No such future awaits this field next to a Super K in the town of Kingsburg, which used to be quite content being known as "the little Swedish village." The farmer has sold out to a developer—hallelujah, say the wife and kids—so another big box might rise.

I cross the Kings, which irrigates more farmland than any river in the world except for the Nile and Indus. In winter, with most permanent crops still in hibernation, there isn't much for the Kings to do. The river, too, falls asleep, bone-dry for long stretches. The snow pack, its lifeblood, hangs heavy on the mountain. Whatever snow has melted waits behind Pine Flat Dam for the call of the irrigation pumps. This is not to say that winter's brown isn't a pretty time. The peach, nectarine and plum trees have been pruned into V-shaped cups, their centers cleared of brush so that they can drink the light. The vines, long canes clipped and tied to wire, won't bud for another month. Hemingway would love these fields.

The sign up ahead reads Traver, but the town no longer exists. It shot up overnight in the late 1800s, a rollicking hamlet with sixteen saloon keepers, eleven blacksmiths, one preacher, one teacher, two physicians, one undertaker, two whorehouses, one Chinese gambling den, two Chinese laundrymen and a Mexican tamale maker named Jesus. Traver held the world record for the greatest amount of wheat shipped from a producing point during a single season. But as fast as it sprouted from the plains, Traver vanished in a cloud of alkali dust, its once fertile soil poisoned by salts bubbling up to the surface.

The road gets wider and the fields flatter in Tulare County. No highway sign proclaims it, but this is the dairy capital of the world. Decades ago, Portuguese farmers from the Azores turned Merle Haggard country into a milk-producing, alfalfa-growing marvel. Now they've been joined by the Dutch families from Chino who sold out their dairies to Southern California builders. Millionaires in their fifties with nothing to do, the Dutch migrate a few hundred miles north to Tulare, building grand houses and even grander dairies.

~*~

Trucks and more trucks. Silverados by the hundreds, caked in mud. I count license plates from Arizona, Nevada, Oregon, Kansas, North and South Dakota and Mississippi. The 2004 World Ag Expo boasts 2.5 million square feet of sold space—exhibits under tents and tin roofs and outdoors on seven thousand cubic yards of bark. The February sun is strong and so are the hats. "Screw Farmers," one cap reads. "Everyone else does." If you're queasy about Mad Cow, this isn't the place for lunch. Even the shish kebab barbecued by the Armenians is beef.

I make my way to the big tractor display on the far side of the Expo and in no time find myself in the crossfire of a debate between Caterpillar and Michelin—with John Deere in the middle. The topic: Which two-hundred-sixty-thousand-dollar tractor leaves the lightest footprint in the field? Every row crop farmer knows that one of the keys to good yields is to keep the soil airy and free from compaction. But with so much ripping and tilling to do, how do you prevent a tractor's tires from pressing down on the soil and nullifying your work?

A decade ago, at this same show, Caterpillar announced the death of the round tire. It had borrowed an idea from the military and turned its tractors into tanks with rubber belts for wheels. No longer did an individual tire bite into the ground. Caterpillars were now powered by a moving track that dispersed the pounds-per-square-inch across a long, wide belt. They called it flotation, a revolution in soil preparation.

But the track must have hit rough ground along the way because the tire—six feet tall and 1,074 pounds—is now front and center at the show. The big Michelin radial is being billed as the ultimate in feather light footprint.

"In terms of soil compaction, a large tire like this is better than the track," the Michelin man says. "If you look at that Caterpillar, the weight is not distributed evenly across the rubber belt. If you have to turn or go on hills, it ruts into the ground. This Michelin can run over your foot and you almost won't feel it."

Flotation, by the way, doesn't come cheap, costing four thousand dollars a tire.

The Cat man, for his part, hands out a slick brochure on the new MT700 series. Any bugs in the old track system have been ironed out over the years, he assures me. The MT700 blends "smooth power delivery and luxurious comfort with unmatched versatility and enduring Caterpillar strength."

I give the boys from Waterloo, Iowa, wearing John Deere green the last word, mostly because they build both kinds of tractors. "It all depends on your soil," one explains. "In the Mississippi Delta where you work the ground wet, the track system wins out. But the tire manufacturers have done a great job building big tires with radial technology. You can't beat them in most situations."

I grab a chicken sandwich and find the tent that's pure carnival: Barbecue grills beside toe rings; Elegant Jewelry by Kathy beside cinnamon-glazed almonds; Good Feet arch support beside Willie's Gopher and Squirrel bait; Calf Growth formula ("Gives Calves More Muscle Than Arnold") beside the California Scarecrow ("No cannons or shotguns, no netting or noise. Just a good old-fashioned scarecrow powered by solar with battery backup").

On the way out, I run into the Sarabian brothers, third-generation grape growers who farm five hundred acres in the Lone Star district east of Fresno. I went to Sunday school with both boys and watched from afar over the years as they struggled with the crankiness of the raisin market. Getting people to eat more sunbaked grapes wasn't easy. The riddle had once occupied the genius of William Saroyan, who mused in a short story that solving the problem was no more complicated than getting every woman in China to place a single raisin in her pot of rice.

Now the Chinese have dammed their own rivers and built a big valley that rivals our valley—grapes, apples, citrus, figs, stone fruits and nuts. Their first full harvest looms just around the corner. The Sarabians, like others, are feeling the heat of a competitor with the same land, the same water and vastly cheaper labor. The brothers have cleared out much of their vineyard land and planted vegetables and pluots, a cross between a plum and an apricot. This year's farm show is a chance to learn about irrigating onions, green beans and cucumbers by drip.

"You stay with the farming long enough and you'll go full circle more than once," David Sarabian says, his chuckle ironic. "What other choice do we have?"

Perhaps in time, a developer will come to their door and lay down another choice. For the time being, they are still farmers.

On the drive home, I think about my father and how things might have been different had he found a way to stay in farming. I'd like to believe he grew disillusioned with suburbia in the early

1970s. He turned his bar into a nightclub and brought in Chuck Berry and other big acts from the city, but it never seemed enough. Early one morning, I was awakened by the sound of shovels and hoes working the soil outside my bedroom window. If my father couldn't return to the farm, he was determined to bring a little farm to North Lafayette Street. He and Grandpa had cleared a quarter of the back-yard and trucked in dirt from the river to add to the hardpan. The three of us spent the day planting tomatoes, peppers, eggplants, cucumbers, watermelons, cantaloupes and squash.

Maybe because the soil was virgin or maybe because I fol-lowed so intently my Grandpa's instructions—"Irrigation is art. Not so much, not so little"—but you should have seen that garden. From July to December, I picked baskets of red and green and purple veg-etables and washed and polished each one. Grandpa said he had never seen such a bounty. Next year, he promised, would be even better. Then the first frost came and the green leaves withered and my father went to work one Sunday night and was shot and killed by two men. It would take more than thirty years for the police to find one of them. My mother didn't live to see the day. The trial left so many questions.

Every year, when my wife isn't looking, I take out another strip of grass or dig another hole in the flower bed to plant my crops. A Chocolate Persimmon in '93. A Muscat vine in '94. A Sun Crest peach in '95. A Black Mission fig in '97. A Mandarin citrus in '98. Lemon Boy tomatoes, Bulgarian tomatoes, Armenian eggplants, Japanese cucumbers. As another orchard gets plowed under out there, I plant another pomegranate or apricot tree back here. I know it's futile, but my garden is now ample and year-round, and the dirt under my nails is honest farm dirt. The country, as my mother used to call it, is right outside my window.

Mark Arax is the co-author of the 2003 bestseller, *The King of California* and author of *In My Father's Name*. He graduated from Fresno State University before receiving a master's degree from Columbia University. He began his journalism career at the *Baltimore Evening Sun* and then returned to California to work for the *Los Angeles Times* in 1984.

Arax is based in Fresno and writes about the life and culture of California's Great Middle for the *Times*.

www.markarax.com.

transients in paradise

by Aimee Liu

Cities, like dreams, are made of desires and fears . . .

This quote, from Italo Calvino's *Invisible Cities,* troubles me as I stroll past the twinkling emporia and ersatz palaces that stereotype the city where I live. At first glance, Beverly Hills seems a dream spun entirely out of desire. If not craving for grandeur, what can explain these many mansions shaped like Versailles . . . or the White House . . . or Hadrian's Villa? If not hunger for beauty, what lies beneath the tucked, lifted, plumped and painted flesh of this town's trademark denizens? Desire illuminates the parades of tourists who crane for glimpses of superstars. It ignites the storefront diamonds and couturier designs. It surely makes the grass grow greener and the squirrels run slower and fatter. Even rats will not be moved in a city where objects of desire are actually closer than they appear. Here garbage bins are studded with discarded filet mignon, gardens ripen with unpicked fruit, and toddlers dressed in

29

Tartine et Chocolat toss croissant crumbs to the birds. Desire sated reinvents itself up and down the food chain, transforming hunger into ambition, envy, lust and greed. Hummers and Porsche Cayennes now dwarf Mercedes as the vehicles *du jour*. Multimillion-dollar deals become the measure of lunch at Spago. And even the most up-to-date mansions "require" annual renovation. Along the central boulevards of Rodeo and Beverly Drive the lines of palm trees stretch and shimmer like soldiers saluting the spirit of longing that spawned this urban paradise, but their lengthening shadows point to desire's doppelgänger—fear.

Contrary to that first glance, the current between desire and fear runs hard through Beverly Hills. I feel it crackle as I watch whole families of orthodox Jews risk death, jayrunning across Santa Monica Boulevard to temple every Saturday. And again as I stand transfixed in my driveway while a husband and wife down the street scream bloody curses at each other, their gilt and granite kitchen not, as they seem to think, soundproof. I sense it when I pass the Persian fathers, exiles from Iran, teaming up for games of Sunday basketball behind Hawthorne elementary school. And in the wizened, hand-holding couples who emerge from once fashionable split-levels that today's speculators will tear down overnight—homes of fifty years. More colorfully, it illuminates the diagonal lipstick and orange cotton candy hair of the antique ladies on Crescent Drive, inching along on their walkers.

The wattage of that current is transience. Who is coming? Who is going? Who is staying, and for how long? A town like Beverly Hills puts up an impressive front of permanence, but no matter how massive the houses, how opulent the stores, how established the brokers of power and fame, or how deep their pockets, the truth of this place is as variable as the traffic passing down Wilshire Boulevard. I see buses carrying housekeepers from Crenshaw nudge the pickups of gardeners from Inglewood, Range Rovers driven by trophy wives cut off Hondas bearing handicap placards. Precious few of the drivers were born here, and nearly as few will die here, there being no hospitals in Beverly Hills, and many started from as far away as Guatemala, Vermont, or Taiwan—or equally distant locales that only appear closer on the map.

As if to prove the point, a white stretch SUV limousine turns the corner and pulls up alongside the public restrooms on upper Beverly Drive. Out spills a hip-hop wedding party—full black tie and satin—and while their bodyguard, glittering with gold, waits leaning against the hood, four pretty girls tumble squealing into one set of toilets and four tough boys hike up their tuxedos and saunter into the other. It is noon under brilliantly clear sunny skies, but the bodyguard's watchfulness makes me walk faster. I think, surely, whatever that he is anticipating must be one of the fears Italo Calvino had in mind, but I'll bet it's not one the original city fathers here ever dreamed of. When the pit stop is over, the wedding party piles back into the limo and makes a circuit of the park, leaning out the windows, the girls trailing chimes of laughter that echo down the street like a taunt.

The chimes land unceremoniously in the shopping cart of a homeless man waiting to cross at the light. He is one of dozens who make up yet another stream of traffic that tells the truth of Beverly Hills. Like hobos and madwomen in the Garden of Eden, they wander among the millionaires shopping at Prada, Armani, and Barneys who respond with selective blindness. They curl up to sleep in the doorways of day spas where society wives get dyed and waxed. They beg for change in front of restaurants where the average tab for two at lunch is more than a hundred dollars. They talk to imaginary lovers while passing young men on hands-free cell phones talking to presumably real amours, and both appear equally mad.

We are all transients of one kind or another. On our way into or out of wealth, into or out of sanity, beauty, love, health, or death.

I listened to some of this city's rich and beautiful at a funeral recently, and their talk bespoke these passages. The daughter of the woman who had died, the daughter's husband, and two family friends were comparing notes on their personal training regimens, flexing their biceps and pushing up sleeves, and asking their fellow mourners to judge which of them was most "buff."

I think of this conversation as I walk past Nate 'n' Al's Deli where, for years, a man who was not one of the city's rich and beautiful used to station his wheelchair. His name was Richard. On weekends he would compete with a smartly dressed woman who parked her wheelchair directly in front of the deli door. She called passersby "Dear" and "Darling" and collected for Jewish charities. Richard was not neatly dressed, and he was his own charity. He wore camouflage greens that swam on him, let his hair go and sometimes his beard grow. Scruffy, you thought on first passing. But his face was keen and alert. I stopped to talk because of the books he read when business was slow. Norman Mailer, Henry Kissinger, Gore Vidal—texts of history and war. If you asked his opinion about those books he'd tell you straight, with confidence and reasoned conviction. He'd look you in the eye as he spoke, and didn't shy from shaking hands. But Richard had a degenerative disease that was shrinking him inside that camouflage.

When he stopped showing up outside Nate 'n' Al's I wasn't the only one who missed him. Within weeks an article appeared in the *Los Angeles Times*. Once, it seemed, Richard had been an aspiring screenwriter, actually had a script optioned. This sci-fi political thriller had made him a number of Hollywood connections, but lack of family and the progression of his disease disabled and distorted his fate. He wasn't technically homeless. He lived in a single-room occupancy hotel located in downtown L.A., from which he "commuted" by bus each day, along with housekeepers, nannies, and nursemaids, to work in Beverly Hills. The hotel manager found him alone in bed the morning he died.

If Richard had had a funeral I doubt his mourners would have spent much talk on personal trainers, but surely there would have been some equivalent version of schadenfreude. Poor bastard, yes, but better him than me.

And there you have the essential current between desire and fear. Desire is merely the version that says, I want and am taking mine—*and better me or us than them or you.* While the inverse, *better him or her or them than us,* is simple code for fear.

Consider: Though it boasts one of the best-armed, -trained, and -paid police forces in the nation, Beverly Hills has no high-rises, no settled slums or tenements, no garbage dumps, junkyards or cemeteries. Like a spoiled and vainglorious daughter, it tries to disguise its fear as a victory for desire by exporting its telltale refuse, sickness, and poverty to its mother metropolis, Los Angeles. And Los Angeles, which long ago was forced to surrender such pretenses, nevertheless so cherishes the illusions this favored child keeps alive that for generations now it's accepted the offal and absorbed its child's

worst fears. But as in Calvino's invisible cities of Beersheba and
Leonia, the tide of mortality, of discarded Chanel bags, rejected tal-
ent, stale newspapers and abandoned trumpets, neglected children,
wasted beauty, used condoms and hypodermics, broken hard drives,
fungal magnolias, dead batteries, and forgotten diaries just keeps rising and washing back over the pristine borders that, in the end, con-
tain nothing.

We are all transients, whether we've lived here for three
hours, or spent a whole charmed life here; whether we're accidental
transplants, or schemed and lied our way in; whether we love this El
Dorado, as the city's official Web site calls it, or whether we choke
on its affluence; whether we plan to leave tomorrow or sink roots
here for generations, none of us is less temporary than the girl now
squatting in front of Starbucks who resembles anyone's niece,
though no one here has ever seen her before. She crouches under a
black woolen poncho and holds up a cardboard sign that reads in
hand-lettering: "Sick, Pregnant, Stranded."

I think of Richard as I watch the streams of perfumed shoppers ignoring the girl's existence. I think of the gold-encrusted guard
keeping watch over that hip-hop wedding party, and the mourners
obsessed with muscle. I think of Calvino's closing paragraph and how
perfectly it captures my struggle with this city where I live:

> *The inferno of the living is not something that will be; if*
> *there is one, it is what we already have, the inferno*
> *where we live every day, that we form by being together.*
> *There are two ways to escape suffering it. The first is easy*
> *for many; accept the inferno and become such a part of*

it that you can no longer see it. The second is risky and demands constant vigilance and apprehension: seek and learn to recognize who and what, in the midst of the inferno, are not inferno, then make them endure, give them space.

Aimee Liu is the author of *Flash House* (2003), a tale of suspense and Cold War intrigue set in Central Asia. She also has written two other novels, *Cloud Mountain* (1997) and *Face* (1994). Her novels have been translated into more than a dozen languages.

Liu published an acclaimed memoir of anorexia nervosa, *Solitaire* (1979), at the age of twenty-five. She has worked as an associate producer for NBC's *Today* show, co-authored seven nonfiction books on medical and psychological topics and is past president of the national writers' organization PEN Center USA West. Liu teaches creative writing at UCLA Extension and lives in Beverly Hills.

www.aimeeliu.net.

showing off the owens

by T. Jefferson Parker

Recently I had a chance to show off California's Lower Owens River to savvy New York angler and novelist Brian Wiprud. I was very proud for the opportunity because I love the temperamental Owens and Brian had never seen it.

It was dead of winter, cool and clear when we ditched the Left Coast Crime Conference in Pasadena and backtracked so we could drive Highway 395. As we passed the beautiful snowcapped San Gabriel Mountains I pointed out that right up there, less than twenty minutes away by car, you could catch wild rainbow trout.

"How big?" asked Brian.

"Six to ten inches. Most in the six range, actually. I caught one a foot long once."

"Hmmm."

Brian—who had recently returned from a fly-fishing tour of the Amazon River—didn't seem impressed.

You know the drive up 395, a classic California highway. We sped through Adelanto with its motel sign announcing "Free Television," left that city's checkered past in the rearview and zoomed into the Mojave Desert. The speedometer hits eighty but you feel like you're standing still. The day is bright and sunny and the windows of your truck are cold.

"What was that In-N-Out Burger back there?" asked Brian. "Is it a chain?"

"Good burgers," I said.

"I don't know, the 'out' kind of worries me."

We slowed through the brief, crumbling towns of Red Mountain and Johannesburg. Then flew past Ridgecrest and the Naval Weapons Center, of which I have fond memories from my boy-hood—weekend family trips built around my father's work at China Lake. I remember three things about Ridgecrest: the scalding heat, the cool blue shimmer of the motel pool, and a stunningly beautiful yet vicious collared lizard my brother and I caught and later tossed into the swimming pool to see if it could swim. (It could.) Continue on 395 and next thing you know, you're starting up the backside of the Sierra Nevada mountains.

Gradually the south end of the Owens River trickles into view. It isn't much to see at first and I bemoan again the Los Angeles Department of Water and Power's theft of the Owens River water many decades ago for their thirsty city far to the south. One of the families living there in Los Angeles and using that water was mine. The Owens was once a mighty river that held mighty fish. Now it is not. However, DWP does keep parts of the reduced Owens open for anglers, so I choose to be an optimist and tell myself that the river is half full. Brian sees the river, sits upright and stares like a retriever spotting a covey of quail by the road.

Now is a good time to digress very briefly on the topic of fly-fishing. It's a progressive disease, like rabies, that starts with an innocuous bite then lies dormant. The bite might be a fish you were lucky enough to catch, might be the beauty of a river or the mountains around it, might even be a movie you saw (to this day fly-fishers bemoan *A River Runs Through It* for all the people it drew into the sport). However the bug gets into you, it lodges, digs in, then begins to grow. My exposure dates back a decade or so, but the obsessive phase of fly-fishing came on slowly, beginning three or four years ago. I won't bore you with symptomatic tales except to say that I can't walk past the koi pond at Fashion Island without wanting to rig up and cast into it; I can't strip a length of dental floss from the box without thinking of leaders and tippets and double-hauls; I spend happy hours standing in my driveway (miles from the nearest river) casting hookless flies to the lizards for practice. (I've caught many.) My case of fly-fishing is in an early stage but I have no hope for a cure. Not to bludgeon the comparison but, like rabies again, the only cure for fly-fishing, once it has reached a certain point, is death.

It was about this time on 395 that Brian first noticed the rash on his hand. It was a raised range of red that looked a lot like poison oak. Figuring there wasn't much poison oak back at the Pasadena Hilton, we agreed it was something in his dinner or breakfast. Brian cracked that it may have been caused by the color of my Explorer, which he ungenerously labeled "butterscotch." (In fact, it's a mystical, totemic blend of orange and gold.) I let that go.

Lone Pine, Independence and Big Pine are the five most

anxious words in the English language because they mean you're getting close to the river. Those last forty-something miles to the Wild Trout section of the Lower Owens River can almost kill an angler. Overhead, Mount Whitney vies majestically for your attention, and Manzanar calls to you in its soft dark voice, but really all you can think about is whether to start by fishing dry flies that float, or go straight to underwater nymphs or streamers in the cold river water. Conversation dwindles into sentence fragments.

We finally made Bishop. We were on the frigid water by noon. The sky was gunmetal gray and the parched red flanks of the canyon angled down to the blue jewel of river flowing hard to the south. I looked down into that water and pictured the thousands of trout down there, unwilling to be caught. I thought of something director Robert Altman recently said: "I love fishing. You put that line in the water and you don't know what's on the other end. Your imagination is under there."

Your imagination, yes. And more than that. The poetry of the actual, for starters. The foliage is flat gold under the brooding gray sky. The river is high-gloss black. A rainbow trout takes an elk hair caddis, explodes through the surface in a spray of bright silver and the entire world holds its breath and watches.

Or maybe just we do.

By dark Brian had caught nine fish and I had caught two. We sat in the dirt by my Explorer and fought free of our waders and boots. I was happy that the Owens had been generous to him, but because he'd out-fished me so effortlessly and insulted the color of my truck, I was secretly pleased that his rash had spread up past both elbows.

"Looks nasty," I said.

"It doesn't hurt. It just itches."

Brian's mother taught him to cast flies when he was a child. Brian took to the sport very early and has fished, studied fishing and written about fishing ever since. He's a great angler. I've seen him show guides how to catch fish on their own rivers—rivers he's never fished before—when they weren't able to. But he's an admittedly vague and ineffectual teacher.

"So Brian, how do you do that double-haul?"

"I don't know. I just do it."

"How did you get those browns to hit the streamers?"

"I don't know. They just did."

And so forth.

After dinner the rash had crept to his shoulders so we sped to the supermarket for remedies: cortisone cream, Vaseline ointment, aspirin, and rubber gloves for his inflamed hands. We tossed in some beer and chips for late-night snacks and a tabloid for entertainment. The checkout clerk was a huge man, very similar in appearance to Chief Broom in the movie *One Flew Over the Cuckoo's Nest*. And just like Broom, he glared at us, glared at our tiny purchases as he swept them over the scanner with his big hands, then glared at us again before he said, in a very deep and clear voice:

"Doesn't look good, guys."

⸎

We met our guide, Tom Loe, at the bridge at eight o'clock the next morning. Tom is an affable but intense young man who has been a commercial fisherman all his adult life. He was fishing the Atlantic when the *Perfect Storm* hit, and lost one of his crew members in the fury of that storm. He has caught everything from huge sharks for restaurants that want them for wall-mounted decorations, to the swordfish they serve for dinner. "But if I were fishing for fun, I'd be after these trout," he said.

We clambered into his boat. A white-bearded, longhaired, old man huddled under up under the bridge wished us a good day of fishing. He had the look of someone who spent a lot of time right exactly there, and I wondered how many troll jokes he'd heard in his life.

Tom was one of the first guides to discover how to catch Lower Owens trout in cold water, from a boat, and in large numbers. Other area guides try to co-opt his method. The basic tool is a sinking-tip flyline loaded with any one of the wonderful streamers that Tom ties himself. The streamers imitate small fish—mosquito fish, to be exact—which trout seem unable to resist when jigged upstream, from behind them. The trout hit them fast and hard. No sipping, hesitation or any attempt at good table manners. Forty-something trout later there was nothing left of Tom's neat little fly but a hook with a bedraggled platoon of feathers stuck to it. But it was still catching fish. Now it dangles from the mirror of my truck as a lucky charm.

We stopped late for lunch, bolted our food and got in a few more hours before the rain started down.

Back in town we stopped in at the Inyo Council for the Arts to see the art exhibit and say hello to our friend, executive director Lynn Cooper. Then across the street to Spellbinder Books, where we talked books a while with owner Ginnie Traver. Spellbinder is a wonderful store. I bought a book about, well, fly-fishing.

By the time we made Whiskey Creek Restaurant for martinis and dinner, Brian's rash had stopped dead in its tracks. Maybe it was the cortisone cream, gloves and aspirin. Or the tabloid. Or the lucky fly dangling from the truck mirror or the art exhibit or the bookstore. Maybe it was the fifty fish he caught. He came back from the restaurant bathroom with a mystified but slightly disapproving look on his face, like he'd been asked to give back something interesting.

"It was the color of my truck that cured you," I said.

We drank a toast to that idea.

Back at the Creekside Inn there was nothing to do but watch TV or read. After a few hours of that I drifted off to sleep, minor rhythms of the boat still in me.

Early the next morning I wandered outside to check the water. The Creekside Inn is actually built around Bishop Creek, which is chaperoned through the grounds by a gentle concrete ditch. In the creek are trout.

I stood by the creek and gazed down at the fish finning in the faint light while the tremendous white Sierra Nevada gazed down on me from the west.

T. Jefferson Parker was born in Los Angeles and has lived all his life in Southern California. His twelve novels, including *Laguna Heat*, *Little Saigon*, *The Blue Hour*, *Cold Pursuit* and *California Girl* all deal with life and times in his native state.

Parker's book *Silent Joe* won the Edgar Award for best mystery in 2001, as well as the *Los Angeles Times* Book Prize for best mystery.

www.tjeffersonparker.com.

the distant cataract about which we do not speak

by Mary Mackey

T he air is full of drifting cottonwood seeds; the water is turning from translucent green to puddled copper; it is 105
degrees Fahrenheit; and once again I am about to sneak up
on the ducks disguised as one of their own. Donning a blue baseball
cap and a pair of sunglasses, I slip into the river, sink until my nose
is just above the surface, and begin to do a slow, underwater breast-
stroke toward a flock of mallards.

The water comes from Sierra snowmelt that has been held
behind Folsom dam like a cache of liquid ice. Even in mid-July, it is
still so cold, it takes my breath away, but over the years I have learned
that, if I grit my teeth and keep swimming, my body will gradually
acclimatize.

The mallards do not notice my approach. They never do.
Perhaps ducks are nearsighted, perhaps they have a limited ability to
sort out foreground and background, perhaps they are too busy
dunking under to grab a beak-full of duckweed, or perhaps they just

don't give a damn. I have never been sure why they always fail to notice the weird thing moving toward them, particularly on days like today when I approach against the current. Logically, I cannot possibly be a log or even a lost beach ball.

I swim nearer. No one looks up. The mallards continue to quack and duck their heads under the water. Over to the left, a male is engaged in a display of splashing and wing beating aimed at impressing a female who appears to be more interested in grooming her tail feathers. I take a few more strokes and float silently into the middle of the flock. The water is so clear I can see tadpoles scattering beneath me in all directions. The shadow of a large fish, a carp perhaps, slides under my feet. I am now close enough that I could reach out and grab the legs of the nearest drake, but I am a duck-observer, not a duck-eater.

For a moment, I relish my presence among them. Again, I wonder why they are not seeing me. Does the bill on my baseball cap make me look like a large mallard? Does their universe include the possibility of a bright blue duck with no eyes or tail feathers?

Suddenly, a female with six tiny ducklings trailing behind her paddles toward me, freezes and does a double take. *That THING is definitely not a duck!* She gives a terrified squawk and my cover is blown. Instantly, all hell breaks loose. Quacking in panic, the ducks scatter like swimmers who have just realized that the log floating toward them is actually a crocodile. Most of the flock takes to the air; the mothers lead their ducklings into the reeds and disappear.

Finding myself alone again with only a few floating feathers to keep me company, I turn and begin to swim back toward the island, still keeping a low profile. Sometimes on the return trip, I see other animals. I cannot get anywhere near the four-foot tall blue herons who are too smart and much too wary to be taken in; but once a green heron actually perched on my cap for a moment, perhaps mistaking me for a small, blue island. On another occasion, near dusk, I looked up and there on the bank, staring at me with unguarded curiosity, was a large buck with a fine rack of antlers. Once, only once, I saw a coyote playing catch with a stick.

Only a week ago as I swam in a warmer backwater, something sneaked up on me. It was not, thank goodness, a rattlesnake. I have only seen one of those in the seventeen-some years I have been coming here and one was enough to last a lifetime; but it gave me quite a start nevertheless. I was swimming under the cottonwoods toward a patch of ripe blackberries that can only be pillaged by water, when I heard a huge smack behind me. I did exactly what the ducks do under such circumstances: I squawked and began to paddle toward safety only to discover that I was sharing the lagoon with a large beaver.

I have no idea why she was out in mid-afternoon. As a rule, beavers are crepuscular creatures. When we paddle our canoe back to the boat launch after sunset, we often encounter as many as twenty of them: large, plump, shadowy balls that slap their tails on the water like a rhythm band as we float by. But this one was up early, and she did not enjoy sharing the lagoon. For a few minutes she swam circles around me, slapping and diving. Then, to my great relief, she slid under water and disappeared. I have never heard of anyone being attacked by a beaver, but I got a good look at her, and just for the record, beaver teeth, when seen up close, are formidable.

But today, I make it back to the island without encountering anything more than a small muskrat and a swarm of Bluetail flies. Stumbling out of the water across a spread of small, unreasonably sharp stones, I towel off, sit down in a lawn chair, pick up the thermos, and pour myself a cup of iced tea. In a few minutes my husband, who originally introduced me to this place, swims up and joins me. We sit, chatting, drinking tea, eating cold melons, and waiting for the sun to set; and in the distance, as always, we hear the sound of The Distant Cataract About Which We Do Not Speak.

Of course, it is not really the sound of a cataract. It is the roar of rush-hour traffic, half of it crossing the Howe Avenue Bridge, half of it crossing the bridge at Watt. We are sitting on an island in the American River, right in the middle of Sacramento, the state capital, a metropolitan area of well over a million people, but my husband and I like to preserve our mutual delusion. We have agreed to imagine we are not a five-minute drive from our home and a twenty-minute walk from the university where we both teach, but instead in some remote part of California where just out of sight a magnificent waterfall foams down into a green pool.

The American River Parkway makes this fantasy amazingly easy. For over thirty miles, it runs through the heart of the city from Folsom Lake to the point where the American River joins the Sacramento. This is a town where if you float in a canoe or sit on an island below the levees you cannot see houses (except in a few places where, alas, the zoning restrictions are being violated). This is a town where some state employees kayak to work; where, no matter how hot it gets, you can get goose bumps and blue lips just by going for a swim.

Over the years, we have seen Hmong families in brightly embroidered, traditional dress picnicking on the banks. We have come upon a circle of Samoans, up to their chests in water, drinking cold beers and singing "Under The Boardwalk" in perfect harmony. When we launch our canoe, we often find ourselves having conversations in Spanish with recent immigrants from Mexico or Central America. About seventy-five thousand Russians live in Sacramento

County, many of them Baptists. We have watched them build huts of reeds and flowers and carry flowered crosses out into the water as part of their baptismal rituals. African-American congregations baptize here too, dressed in white robes. Like the Russians, they sing hymns and pray. I am always moved when I hear them. This, I think, is the spiritual heart of the river.

Once, during a January when it looked as if the levees might break, my husband and I came upon a pile of candy wrapped in gold foil, pineapples and oranges sliced in half, several beheaded guinea fowl, a pack of matches and a handful of popcorn—traditional offerings made to the goddess Oxum by devotees of the African-Brazilian religion Candomblé. On another occasion, we went down to the river to launch our canoe and found the parking lot occupied by a Russian Orthodox priest and his congregation. The priest appeared to be blessing the river with incense. A procession made its way to the edge of the river bearing banners painted with holy icons. I believe their prayers were in Old Slavonic.

But nothing can compare to a night in early August when my husband and I came to the river and found it full of small, floating lanterns. A Japanese priest stood at the boat launch chanting as the lanterns drifted toward him and his congregation. We found out later that this is a traditional ceremony for souls lost at sea, but that now it is done to commemorate those who died at Hiroshima and Nagasaki in August of 1945. Above the lanterns, a full moon rose into the sky, bright and large as a second sun. The flames swirled in the current, the night primroses blossomed, the beavers were silent, and for a few moments the American was a river of light.

Mary Mackey's published works include four volumes of poetry (*Split Ends, One Night Stand, Skin Deep* and *The Dear Dance of Eros*); a novella (*Immersion*); and nine novels (*McCarthy's List; The Last Warrior Queen; A Grand Passion; Season of Shadows; The Kindness of Strangers; The Year The Horses Came; The Horses at the Gate; The Fires of Spring;* and *The Stand In.*). Her tenth novel is *Sweet Revenge* (Kensington, 2004) and her fifth collection of poetry is *Breaking The Fever* (Oso Books, 2004).

Mackey is a professor of English and writer in residence at California State University in Sacramento, where she teaches creative writing and film. She also writes under the pen name Kate Clemens.

www.marymackey.com.

ode to caltrans

by Héctor Tobar

In this dream I am standing over the Hollywood Freeway and the traffic runs backwards. The Suburbans race in the direction of their taillights, young men cling from the overpasses and swallow up the scribbles on the road signs into graffiti-erasing cans. The 6 P.M. bumper-to-bumper up over the Cahuenga Pass runs southward into downtown, where teams of skilled technicians slowly dismantle the Cathedral overlooking the freeway, covering the site with an asphalt parking lot. Eventually the traffic thins and the concrete roadway loses its tar-colored stains and returns to the pristine gray of its youth. The cars begin to shrink in size, as do their drivers, until man and woman and machine fit inside the lanes better. The Hollywood Freeway becomes the newer highway I remember from my youth, curves sculpted around hillside neighborhoods of bungalows and apartments on stilts, a roadway starting to show signs of its age but not yet bursting at the seams. The exit signs that have borne faithful witness to the coming and goings of my California life—to breakups and funeral processions, to marriage and birthday caravans—lose their sooty patina and glow in the understated CalTrans green in which they were minted. I look at the signs, the phallic arrows, the sans-serif font announcing destinations—Hollywood Blvd., Vermont Ave.—and feel the Switzerland-like orderliness and simplicity that inspired their design. I am eight years old again, staring out the window of my parents' sky-blue 1969 Volkswagen Beetle, listening to the climbing sound of my father shifting gears, taking in the new-car smell, looking for the statue by the Silver Lake underpass, the one of the exterminator with the mallet preparing to smash a roach about as big as an eight-year-old boy.

When you live far away from California, as I have for the past three years, you begin to appreciate the freeway for the essential idea behind its construction—that automobiles should inhabit their own universe, segregated from the slower forms of locomotion. In other countries I've visited, cars and pedestrians live incestuously. You can drive ninety kilometers per hour on what looks like a freeway around the edge of Montevideo, Uruguay, for example, and still have to dodge street vendors spiriting across your field of vision and horse-drawn carts merging from the onramp to the number-three lane. In Iraq, the super highways Saddam built are a kind of Middle Eastern tribute to CalTrans. The undulating zinc center dividers of the Baghdad freeways are the same as those running through Santa Monica and the functional, gravity-defying concrete overpasses are engineering cousins to those designed on drafting tables in Sacramento. Given the palm trees and Baghdad's insistently dun landscape, you could easily believe you somehow had been transported to Barstow, except, of course, for the large number of Bradley Fighting Vehicles cruising in the fast lane, and the peculiar habits of the local drivers. Iraqis often will take a one-hundred-kilo-meter-per-hour southbound detour on the northbound lanes to avoid the craters cut into the roadway by American ordinance, plunging into the oncoming traffic as if that were a perfectly normal thing to do. In California we drive too fast, but at least there are enforceable rules; there is a logic and highway etiquette respected by eighty-five percent of the driving public and enforced by a relatively incorrupt-ible Highway Patrol. If the Buenos Aires commuters who make a habit of straddling the dotted lines on the Highway of the Sun tried the same thing on the Santa Monica, they would either be pulled over for a roadside sobriety test or find themselves targets of road-rage jus-tice. In Los Angeles, we don't suffer traffic fools well, because we drive almost as much as we breathe; we understand that the hours we spend outside the shell of our vehicles are mere episodes between the daily freeway slog. The Law of Evolution has dictated our adaptation into *homo californius mobilius*, and clever tool-making—the hands-free cellular phone, the multi-CD player, and the radar detection device—has saved our breed from extinction.

~※~

When my first and second sons were born I did not take the freeway. I had become, by that time, too aware of the metal-crunching bedlam on the Pasadena Freeway, which was the main link between my home in Mount Washington and the hospital where my wife's ob-gyn worked. Winter was an especially frightening time to be on the One-Ten, as the California neophytes call it: Once I wit-nessed a sports car flip in the air on the long curve where Arroyo

Seco Boulevard ends and the freeway begins. The car twisted in the air like a gyroscope before landing right side up, its driver staring out at me, his eyes empty in shock. I mouthed the words "Are you okay?" as I drove past, but he didn't answer. Another night, I inched to the end of a mile-long bumper-to-bumper back up only to see a man's body hanging limply, and unmistakably dead, outside the driver-side window of an accordion-pressed pickup truck. Every morning brought a new rip to the chain-link fencing that separated the free-way from the streets beyond, where bits of glass and pieces of amber taillights garnished the asphalt and grass. People were simply driving too fast, in cars that were too big for the narrow lanes in the most ancient of our freeways. When my wife went into labor, I took the side streets.

I hadn't been so cautious when I turned thirty and decided I would ask my future wife to marry me, speeding along those same sinuous lanes toward the Bridewell Avenue exit in South Pasadena with a dozen red roses on the front seat of my pickup truck and thinking that "Bridewell" had to be a good omen. I was rushing toward my future along roads tended, since my birth, by CalTrans workers in Day-Glo orange vests who toiled day and night to keep my path free of obstacles, and to make the roadway as smooth as a carpet of black velvet. Every now and then I became aware of when and where one of these workers was killed; CalTrans placed signs with a picture of a white CalTrans helmet on the roadside, as a poignant and wordless memorial. But then there were too many signs and CalTrans took them down because a highway shouldn't look like a cemetery. I was, then, just becoming aware of the cycles of life and death, and how the flow of traffic sometimes guides us against our will onto the cloverleaf exchanges between our earthly selves and the great highways of the beyond.

A few years earlier, I had driven down the Hollywood Freeway and the Santa Ana to the Los Angeles County Coroner's Office to pick up the belongings of my stepfather. He committed suicide on the green lawns of Rose Hills, overlooking the 605 Freeway, which to me remains the "San Gabriel River Freeway," though not even the mapmakers call it that anymore. My stepfather had shot himself during one of those windswept Thanksgiving weekends, when autumn leaves zip across the lanes of traffic, dancing over bumpers and windscreens, mixing with the plastic and aluminum detritus lifted from the shoulders. In the years since, I have noticed that the same hot winds blow every Thanksgiving weekend. I feel those winds and remember that drive to the coroner's office, in my pickup with my mother at my side looking out across the lanes of traffic, wondering why the man she loved would betray her so.

My mother was my first regular passenger, back when she was a freshly-minted divorcée, and I was a sixteen-year-old apprentice commuter at the controls of her Pinto station wagon, sky-blue with a strip of faux-wood paneling along the side. We lived then in South Whittier, the midway point of the Santa Ana Freeway, and an unfortunate place to begin a daily trek into downtown Los Angeles. Back then—before hundreds of CalTrans employees and contractors toiling countless graveyard shifts had widened it—the Santa Ana was barely a couple of lanes linking downtown to the Matterhorn at Disneyland and Sea World and San Diego beyond. My mother hated the drive north to her job as a keypunch operator and practically celebrated when I got a job in the same building in the summer of 1979 and asked "Can I drive?" This was the summer of my full induction into California adulthood, the lines at the Department of Motor Vehicles and the showdowns with the eyes of foes gazing back at you in rear-view mirrors. I learned to make those last-second, fifty-five-mile-per-hour mental calculations at the spot where one freeway divides into two—"Should I keep going on the Santa Ana, or try going around on the Long Beach instead?"

Long before I had ever put my hands on the wheel, I was learned in freeway cartography. I had a strange and very lonely childhood, part of which I filled by studying the maps of the Southern California highway grid, then still a work in progress, some just visions represented by dotted lines, like the one for the end of the Pomona, which did not yet reach its namesake. I had been out there several times with my father, following the detour signs to the last exit, catching a glimpse of the bulldozers and dump trucks standing on a patch of brand-new roadway. The work crews were preparing to push the freeway past the last ring of suburbs and into the orange groves beyond. On my maps, I looked expectantly at the dotted line of the "Beverly Hills Freeway," which would one day connect Rodeo Drive to East Hollywood, where I lived with my parents before they were divorced: the never-to-be-built Beverly Hills was going to be my personal road to the sea, taking me in twenty minutes from East Hollywood to the cliffs of Pacific Palisades.

Our apartment was a short walk from the corner of Sunset Boulevard and Western Avenue, two blocks from the eight lanes of the Hollywood Freeway. A few times I pedaled my bicycle up to the zinc barrier at the end of our street, to stand over the ivy-covered precipice and look down at the river of moving metal below. The freeway was a canyon of sound, something between wind and rushing water, as if the lanes were rapids filled with canoes that occasionally blasted a horn or screeched brakes. The freeway sounded even more like water a few hundred feet back, when I stood at the window of my third-grade classroom at Grant Elementary. Our school was close enough to the freeway that our ecology-minded teacher made it the subject of a science test: She had us cover a piece of cardboard with Vaseline, which she then placed inside our classroom. She put a second one outside the window facing the freeway. Of course, the Vaseline board facing the freeway turned black a few days later, proof that the river of cars below our classroom was churning up a mist of carbon emissions, little particles that couldn't be good for our eight-year-old lungs.

Perhaps that was the first time I thought of the freeway as a place of pollution and peril. Up to then, it was just the byway of our family wanderings, the Sunset and Hollywood Boulevard onramps, the beginning of most of our visits to relatives and friends. To sit in my father's Volkswagen with my nose pressed to the rear window, watching the traffic flow along with us at fifty miles per hour was as natural to me as walking along the fence posts of a country road would be to a boy from Nebraska. The landmarks of the two miles or so of freeway between my home and the Vermont Avenue exit to the south are engrained in the deepest, most nostalgic and pleasant recesses of my memory. I can close my eyes today and still see the oversized, hopeful sign declaring "McGovern for President" attached to a building on Vermont that rose like a bluff over the freeway; it would later become a night club famous for something called "female mud wrestling." I can remember the smaller brick cube of the workshop of the Earl Scheib at the top of the Santa Monica Boulevard onramp. When I was a toddler in diapers, one of my father's first jobs was at Earl Scheib, a car-painting outfit that could transform your cream-colored Thunderbird into a cherry-colored Thunderbird in the time it took the sky to evolve from morning blue to the desert-dust-and-ash smoothie of midday. My father's task was to hop into the still-moist sedans and station wagons and roll them out of the shop, then down the Santa Monica Boulevard onramp to merge onto the Hollywood Freeway, trying to get the speed up to at least forty in the short drive to the next exit, so that the rush of wind would dry the paint. My father tells me his palms would begin to sweat every time he did this, because he was just a couple of years removed from Guatemala and didn't have a driver's license yet.

My mother and father were car-less for the first year or so after their arrival from Guatemala in 1962. They had no wheels, no independent way to get around, and in 1960s Los Angeles, as in early twenty-first century Los Angeles, this was an especially helpless and pitiful state. How would my pregnant mother make it to the hospital once she went into labor? For years, my mother told me she believed she had transmitted the transportation anxiety of the last days and hours of her pregnancy to me through the placenta, a story I heard often after I became a sad and chubby adolescent; it was, she believed, the root cause of my melancholy. My mother worried about taking the bus to the hospital—*Would they even let a woman in labor on? Would she need exact change?*—until a neighbor in her apartment building came to the rescue. Booker Wade drove my mother to Los Angeles County General Hospital from their apartment off Santa Monica Boulevard, down the Hollywood Freeway to the Santa Ana. I prepared to enter the world inside my mother's womb as she rode in Booker's convertible, the top down because he couldn't get it to close. From the back seat, she looked up through the cold February air at the concrete underbelly of the great Four-Level Interchange, the first nexus of the regional freeway grid, a monument to modernity where buses and tanker trucks could float for a moment or two in the California sky. Here, the Pasadena, Hollywood and Santa Ana freeways and a half dozen "transition roads" crisscrossed in an enormous cement starburst. Booker's car rolled down to the lowest level of the interchange, the "transition" to the Santa Ana.

I wonder if, in that second or two, my mother didn't forget her labor pains and look up and feel a sense of wonder: She had arrived in a country where traffic could fly. Maybe she passed that sense of awe to me, the boy bouncing inside her belly, doing turns inside the amniotic fluid, feeling his mother glide forward at fifty-five miles per hour, and then dip and slow to thirty-five and finally climb up again, accelerating anew.

Héctor Tobar is a Los Angeles-born writer and journalist. The son of Guatemalan immigrants, he was raised in Hollywood and educated in California public schools, including the University of California, Santa Cruz and the University of California, Irvine, where he received a Masters of Fine Arts in Creative Writing. His novel *The Tattooed Solider* (Penguin Books, 1998) was a finalist for the PEN Center USA West Award for Fiction.

Tobar is currently the Buenos Aires Bureau Chief for the *Los Angeles Times* and was a member of the reporting team that won the Pulitzer Prize for coverage of the 1992 Los Angeles riots. His latest work is the nonfiction book *Translation Nation: On the Trail of a New American Identity* (Riverhead Books, 2005).

montalvo, myths and dreams of home

by Thomas Steinbeck

I am justifiably proud to say that, up until now, I have successfully evaded all requests to write a cunning and colorful description of my home, the elusive and ethereal State of California. It's not that I'm perennially bone-lazy (though lethargy must be taken into account), but, rather, I have an abiding attitude that must be ascribed to a selfish reluctance to share my chewing gum with the rest of the class. After all, what rewards could possibly induce me to share the best of my California treasures? Especially possessing, as I do, a certain knowledge that my ultimate reward will be to observe those pristine locations suddenly crowded with ecologically insensitive tourists and their military complement of all-terrain vehicles—each and every explorer, of course, believing their veins gush with the courageous essence of Lewis and Clark and the Corps of Discovery?

But now I suppose age and philosophical resignation have withered my legendary resistance. I've become aware that most people lack the physical dedication required to experience "the world primeval," particularly if it requires protracted discomfort of any kind. Thus, I now feel that mentioning the most moving California vista I know will hardly cause deadly impact. I do so, confident in the knowledge that for the present, these remote mythical landscapes shall go undisturbed by all but the most dedicated searcher. And, by definition, such people are generally deferential and protective of such experiences.

And speaking of searches, I invite the reader to hold fast to the concept of "mythology" for the present. It will prove helpful in the task ahead, for an odd truth remains to be revealed and witnessed. In part, the following meanderings will illustrate that the brilliance and energy of a rational dream inevitably fades, and in nature's season becomes little more than a source-myth to succeeding generations. It's happened before. It's happening now. I present such an example.

T he early fifteen hundreds were remarkably shallow years for the publishing game in Spain. Sanguine religious tracts decrying the doom and torturous punishment of all Protestants were considered steady sellers, of course, but only to a niche market of psychotics predisposed to enjoy that kind of entertainment. But in general, it can be said that the printer's ink was drying up for want of innovation and imaginative new material. And worse yet, the small but dedicated reading public, bored by the common Church-censored fare, was actually having racy French novels and Dutch philosophical treatises smuggled into the country to fill the gap. The Dutch were already publishing seventy percent of all the books in Europe, and they found the Spanish market a perfect place to unload all their seconds and returns.

And then, just as the printer's guilds were beginning to despair, and massive layoffs loomed on the horizon, a cluster of homegrown scribblers decided to take up what appeared to be a lucrative literary challenge. Their reasoning was simple enough. Why struggle through a "purple" romance in French or some other barbarian patois, when one might wade through the same twaddle in a more convenient tongue.

Well, the whole Spanish Romance thing took off like a scalded pig, and in no time everyone in the publishing game was up to his or her castanets in doubloons. The Amadis romances, though simply a coddled adaptation of the Arthurian cycle, found an enthusiastic audience in old Castilia and cemented a trend toward trashy novels that we still appreciate today. This literary novelty also became a fat new target for the Church authorities. And this was very timely, since Spanish cardinals and bishops were running out of weedy heretics to castigate for one thing or another.

To be sure, the light of true genius would not shine until Miguel de Cervantes came on the literary scene some thirty years later with his masterpiece, *Don Quixote*. For it has been well argued that while doing time in the local nick for monetary reasons, he found the leisure to invent the modern Novel.

But in 1510 the literary pickings were bone slim, so obviously the arena was open to all sorts of hacks and literary footpads. But one particular gentleman of superior talents, and a scion of the new wave, was an industrious fellow by the name of Garcia Rodrigues de Montalvo. This semi-scholarly fellow, who had garnered no small reputation as a translator of French romances, decided that writing Spanish versions was easier than scudding off to the New World in search of Incas to rob. With a loan from his agent, a wink from his publisher and the promise of great things to come, Montalvo hunkered down and wrote a thrill-a-minute potboiler entitled *Las Serges De Esplandian*. Well, despite a caustic mauling from the critics at the *Toledo Times* and the *Cadiz Herald*, the book was an instant bestseller among the lesser nobility, and soon an object of moral suspicion for the Church fathers. In short, things were looking up all around.

Like most rehashed literary swill, the very existence of this tit-illating mediocrity would have melted away in the course of events if it hadn't been for the instant popularity of one fascinating detail in Montalvo's yarn. Hidden within the romantic convolutions of the text, was the reinvention of an ancient vision, for Montalvo depicted a lush and fruitful paradise, a utopian island set in the western sea. Though few know or care about the original story, everyone knows the name of Montalvo's "Atlantian" cousin, for he christened his paradise California.

This mythological distillation of numerous classical fantasies charmed the public's need for distraction to such an extent, that even as late as 1533, Cortez and his motley gang of metal-clad head-bashers knew the story well enough to name the longest western peninsula yet discovered after Montalvo's whimsical creation California. It is curious to note that anyone who has traversed the length and breadth of Baja California is left to question the sanity of those sun-baked and addlepated conquistadors.

But this initial miscalculation only endured while Cortez still believed his initial discovery was but a barrier island off the coast of Mexico. To be sure, once those canny Spanish navigators and cartographers discovered their error, they bowed to the discrepancy by renaming their original discovery Baja California and, by ultimately bypassing the original island myth for a more pragmatic continental reality, christened everything to the north, Alta California.

What remains so remarkable about the origin myth of California is that, for a great many people at home and abroad, this romantic indulgence still holds water. Indeed, the very notion that California was, and is, a veritable paradise on Earth, has had many proponents throughout our national history. Certainly Thomas Jefferson wouldn't have sponsored Lewis and Clark if he'd thought stories about the wealth and resources of the western shore were just

so much beaver poop. Jefferson was an astute and well-versed advo-
cate of the Age of Enlightenment, so when he heard that even
Voltaire was harping on the same utopian myth of California, he
decided that land-hungry Americans might stand in need of a generous portion of that pie for themselves. The fantasy of eventual
usurpation was conceived in that instant, though it only found its
stunted, dishonorable maturity with the storming of Mexico City by
Winfield Scott and his band of blue-clad Visigoths.

This septic splinter of American history goes a long way to
buttress the power of Montalvo's utopian invention. Political fortunes
and the blood of thousands of soldiers had now been thrown into the
mix, and the resultant brew only amplified the myth and set it center
stage in the hearts of millions of impulsive and restless searchers.

What impresses the studied observer over a period of time is
the fact that a marginal literary invention from an eminently forgettable
sixteenth-century romance novel should still hold so many people in
thrall to the present day. In a lifetime of travel I have become acquaint-
ed with hundreds of people who dreamed of coming to California. Most
of them couldn't have cared less about the other forty-nine states, for
it was the intricate stratification and emotional significance of the
California myth to which they clung like wide-eyed orphans.

Of course, we hard-strung old natives know better, or at
least think we do, but that's an illusion of no lesser dimensions than
the original myth. For it's a reality that those of us who can remember
the California of forty or fifty years ago cling to our own memory-
myths more tenaciously than anyone else. For recollection will never
allow "old hands" to concede that present myth could hold a match
to the glorious re-imaginings of the past. My fellow pilgrims deem,
and maybe rightly so, that the desperate uncertainties of days gone
by, once survived, hold in our hearts greater consequence than the

ubiquitous mediocrity of contemporary legends.

One might successfully hypothesize the theory that, as allegories go, California is the only state in the Union that has flourished beyond all expectations, primarily because it has always been all things to all people. And like the seduction of the Muses, she always appears in the garb of our own desires, giving each a familiar, loving reflection of one's self. This is a most equitable arrangement if a body is willing, as in marriage, to shoulder the good with the bad. For most people, the heady delights of even a mythical seduction fade with the realities of a new day. But the California Myth has a slippery custom of reinventing itself every time you turn around. Just when you think you've got a handle on the newest fashion (exit stage right), the whole marvel instantly changes costume and reenters stage left. Even for the brightest among us, this constant metamorphic whirl can prove a daunting challenge to keep track of. It's akin to traveling a familiar road, only to find that what had been a lovely pasture last month has been transformed into a full-blown mega-shopping center in an instant. What happened? Where was I when they pulled off that one? It can be a jarring experience to watch one's environment change with such rapidity that the recognizable becomes foreign in the blink of an eye. *Sic transit gloria mundi.* (Thus passes the glory of the world.)

And what should be said of my personal California myth? In one sense, I suppose my version of the parable is more primitive than most. That is to say, no fortunes were ever sought and no dynasties envisioned, principally because such engaging vanities have no rational place in my part of California for the present. Admittedly, my little corner is but a speck on the map, but it has a broad mythical reputation nonetheless. Even my grandmother, Olive Steinbeck, who had a character unsullied by humor or whimsy, knew and respected the magic and power of the locale. This rugged bastion against the

waves has been called various names over the centuries, but few people who weren't raised there would remember them. Instead it has
retained a moniker that is no title at all, but rather a Spanish map
reference. We know it today as The Big Sur, and no other site in
California can claim itself equal in majesty, magic or myth. Perhaps
this will appear a dastardly piece of bias, but I don't care.

In my youth, and in the company of reverent comrades of
like mind, I have ridden horse and mule over its rocky passes, and
camped by mountain streams rich in cress and evening doves. And
then, struggling over that last scrabble buttress of the western mountains, I have been abundantly rewarded by the sight of the great
Pacific, beating foam-crested fists against every rocky intrusion into
its realm. There is nothing I know that compares with the magnifi-
cence of a sunset seen from high in The Big Sur, and nothing as
mysterious and enchanting as riding through the fingerlings of fog as
they trace through the scrub oak up the canyons. If it can truly be
said that one's spirit may be stimulated to accept the sublime by one
location as opposed to another, then for me that place exists high on
the crests and along the rugged cliffs of The Big Sur. Even though I
cannot now call those secluded canyons and cliffs home, my abiding
memories of this lonely span of California coastline holds my soul in
thrall and delights the imagination beyond all else I know.

And while I'm on the subject of myths, The Big Sur is the
only place in California, besides the high Sierras and the Northwest,
where stories of strange and unexplained humanoids abound. The high
mountains, for instance, are the solitary habitat of the great Sasquatch,
a giant man-like creature well known and respected by numberless generations of native peoples. Likewise, according to indigenous tribes like
the Rumsen, who perennially roamed The Big Sur in search of game,
herbs and acorns, related that the more remote areas of their range was

home to a diminutive species of beings that have always been referred to as The Dark Watchers. These creatures were said to be smaller than most humans, extremely shy and never seen in broad daylight. These mysterious beings were never known to intimidate or cause any harm, but one was aware that they were always there in the shadows, unseen and watching everything that transpired in their territory.

There have been a number of modern sightings of these small beings as well. Even my hard-boiled grandmother swore to the existence of The Dark Watchers, and often left them little gifts of fruit and homemade candy in small Chinese baskets as she rode horseback down the coast to teach school. She later disclosed an interesting piece of evidence concerning these little people. On her return journeys north, Olive would find that a beautiful seashell or a bird's feather of great perfection had been placed in the basket in exchange for her gifts. She said that it was always a wonderful surprise to find the baskets just where she had placed them. Of the many she had left in various places, none was ever taken, and each always contained a token of gratitude. Now, there's a whopping fine California myth for you, and I, for one, believe every word. But that's what happens when you're in love.

Thomas Steinbeck is the author of *Down To a Soundless Sea*, a critically acclaimed collection of short stories. After serving in Vietnam, he returned there as a combat photographer, which inspired his interest in documentaries and filmmaking. Since then, he has written and produced numerous screenplays. He also sits on the board of the National Steinbeck Center in Salinas and the Center for Steinbeck Studies in San Jose. Steinbeck is an honorary board member of the Stella Adler Theatre in Hollywood. He lives on the Central Coast of California and is working on his first novel.

the last little beach town

by Edward Humes

Seal Beach's red-tile roofed, hacienda-style City Hall was built in 1929, but lately part of the lower floor has been rented out to a beauty salon to bring the town a bit of extra revenue. Midway through my work on this essay, I had stopped by to ask about the finer points of town history. Joanne Yeo, who has occupied the City Clerk's office longer than anyone can remember, rummaged under the counter and handed me a little book called *A Story of Seal Beach*.

Now, I had popped in on the spur of the moment after a morning walk on the beach—I had on some old jeans and a sweatshirt and I'm not even sure I had shaved—and Joanne didn't know me from Adam. But when I told her I had run out without my wallet and didn't have the five-dollar purchase price on me, and I started to slide the little book back across the counter, she just waved me off and said, "Take it. Come back and pay whenever you get a chance."

Imagine walking into City Hall in L.A. or Santa Monica or

Santa Ana or anywhere else this side of Mayberry and having a clerk (once one finally deigns to saunter over and acknowledge your existence) tell you, *Take it, go ahead, I trust you.* This just does not happen in this century in this part of the world—except, in Seal Beach, it does. This is what we call The Seal Beach Way. This is why few people who stumble on this place ever leave, why Seal Beach gets into their blood, why they move into horrendously overpriced fifties-era tract homes on pint-sized lots and start plotting with architects to add a hideously overpriced extra three hundred square feet of living space—and consider themselves damn lucky to do it. For they have found, tucked inside one of the most heavily urbanized landscapes on Earth, the last little unspoiled beach town in Southern California.

People actually walk here. We leave our cars at home and stroll to the not-Starbucks coffee shop, amble to the Gap-less and Banana Republic-free Main Street, walk our kids to school, or simply put one foot in front of the other until we reach the beach or the market or the playground. Sometimes we even talk to each other along the way, which turns out, after all, not to be unlawful in car-centric SoCal.

Part of the reason Seal Beach has pulled this off is a matter of the company we keep: The town is the first and easiest-to-miss pearl on a string of larger, more prominent beach cities stretching southward into Orange County. It lies at the very top of the chain, abutting the concrete-bedded San Gabriel River that forms a cold, gray border with L.A. County, the famous Orange Curtain. Because Seal Beach lies right on this boundary between the port-city of Long Beach, which years ago trashed its own stretch of coast, and über-Republican, affluent Orange County, non-locals are often confused about exactly which side of the divide claims Seal Beach. The correct answer (philosophically, if not legally) is neither: Seal Beach is proudly not part of L.A.—the town's founding father, Phillip Stanton, formerly speaker of the California Assembly, made sure of that ninety years ago. But it also shares little in common with the planned communities, condo canyons, conservative activism and housing covenants commonly associated with "the OC" (nobody outside of Hollywood scriptwriters and preternaturally attractive twenty-something actors pretending to be teenagers actually calls it that, by the way). You can plaster your garage with a rainbow-hued seascape mural or paint your stucco walls flaming purple or erect a strangely large scale model of a lighthouse on your front lawn and the taste police will not knock on your door here. Seal Beach is militantly untrendy.

Confusion about Seal Beach's identity and location is key to its survival—people who live twenty minutes away aren't quite sure where or what it is, and once you hit the geographically fashionable zones of West L.A., you might as well say you live on the Yucatan—it would never occur to those folks, happily for us, to drive those forty-five minutes south to Seal.

The favored destinations are the beach cities to the south splayed out along the Pacific Coast Highway: Huntington Beach, Newport Beach, Laguna Beach—bigger and better known, all of them, though each has abandoned its roots over time. Huntington Beach replaced its surfer-shack charms with a look best described as Vista del Condo. Newport Beach has become the world's most picturesque outdoor shopping mall and Mercedes dealership. The funky artists' enclave that was Laguna Beach remains the most strikingly beautiful of the lot, homes perched on coastal hillsides in perfect tribute to Mediterranean villas, but the quest for tourist dollars has made its downtown a grid-locked parking lot, and chain-store creep is pushing out personality for purchase power.

Then there is Crystal Cove, which occupies the magical stretch of coastline between Newport and Laguna, one of the main reasons I moved to California. I had flown in for a job interview, my head jammed with a childhood's worth of mythic images accumulated while growing up on the East Coast in the sixties, when the idea of California and paradise were synonymous, all red convertibles and Beach Boys and surfer girls and pale blue skies melting into white-sand beaches. My collision with reality came in 1985, when pollution here was at its historical worst; my naïveté did not survive my very first descent into the Los Angeles Basin. I watched my plane enter a layer of air the color of an old teabag and I just wanted to cash in my ticket and go home. It only got worse when I rented a car, heading south on Pacific Coast Highway starting in Long Beach. I saw a coastal strip marred by one fast-food restaurant and gas station and cheap motel after another.

But then I rounded a curve and the broken promise vanished along with my breath. Stretching out below me was the landscape I had expected, but better: On the inland side, green and brown hills, studded with a few wind-tortured trees and cut by a rugged canyon, rose up from the coastal plain, a heard of cows grazing in the distance. To the right, a graceful, curving arc of frothing Pacific chewed at a virgin white beach pocked with tide pools, and tucked into low, green cliffs, a tiny village of thirties-era bungalows overlooking the water—not mansions, just drafty little houses meant to be used and scraped and repainted year after year in the harsh salt environment, looking as natural here as pieces of driftwood. Back then, visitors parked on the inland side of PCH, then walked through a tunnel under the highway, a glorified culvert, really, and when you emerged on the other side to the sound of waves crashing, the sensation was of having traveled back in time. And seeing that, seeing my mythic California hadn't been paved over entirely, I knew I could move here after all. If there could still be a Crystal Cove, I reasoned, there could still be other traces of treasure spared the axe and bulldozer.

Right.

Today Crystal Cove is a strip mall and a golf course and stack of carefully coiffed and color-coordinated mansions overlooking the non-native vegetation and palms imported to replace the uprooted natural landscape. The beach houses were sold to the state, which promptly kicked all the renters out of their rapidly vanishing paradise, although the grandiose and ludicrous plans to turn the historic old cottages into some sort of luxury hotel never came to pass. Government officials nonetheless congratulated themselves on this abomination, because the landowner, the insatiable Irvine Company, agreed to dedicate a strip of the once-pristine inland pasture and canyon for park use. It serves more as a reminder of what's been lost than a preservation of the cove's past splendors; I find myself avoiding that drive I once sought any excuse to make.

During that fateful drive in 1985, I passed through Seal Beach without noticing its charms, or even noticing it at all. This is because the Coast Highway cuts inland here, three long blocks from the sand, so all you see is an unremarkable succession of gas stations, a strip center, some shops—nothing to pull you in and get you to stop. The heart of Seal Beach, its Old Town section, is hidden from view, but the mile-long stretch of beach neighborhood between the San Gabriel River and Anaheim Bay is a gem. It easily mixes old bungalows with newer-money mini-mansions, throwing together original owners who bought in for nine thousand dollars after the war with newcomers who wish their property taxes were that low. Once I discovered Seal Beach, years after moving to the area, stumbling on another surviving piece of original California, I was hooked.

⚓

The center of Old Town is Main Street, a true old-fashioned downtown, where most of the businesses are locally owned and the fanciest restaurant's only dress requirement is shirt and shoes. Business is conducted in shorts and T-shirts; the local congressman can be seen now and then yakking on his cell in his wet suit after surfing.

At the foot of Main Street is the Seal Beach Pier, and the stretch of sand on either side of it is broad and flat and mostly empty. It's a south-facing beach, and the best time to see it, my favorite time, is early afternoon on a winter day. When the sun is as high as it's going to get, it's still slightly in front of you, so that it dazzles the eye when you stare straight out at the water, Catalina Island hazy in the distance, the handful of figures surfing the pier reduced to mere silhouettes. The water becomes monochromatic in this light, a pattern of gray and white circlets, moving sinuously, like scales on a reptile's skin, rippling and sparking in the sunlight, the waves so close together it's impossible to differentiate them, their sound merging into one sustained hiss, the reptile's mesmerizing sigh. Except for sunny summer weekends, the beach is so wide it is possible to be lonely here, to feel small, to not hear the Nokia song chiming in someone's pocket.

It was not always this way. Seal Beach started where its sister beach towns have ended up, the first town served by the Red Car Line, bringing in the beach-bound hordes beginning in 1904. City father Stanton rounded up a pool of investors and built the longest pleasure pier on the West Coast, with fifty-two giant "scintillators" left over from the most recent world's fair erected at the end. These huge light standards, arrayed like a battalion of soldiers staring out to sea, cast brilliant rainbows of light onto the water for night swimming. By 1920, the Jewel Café and the Seal Beach Dance Pavilion and Bathhouse with its ninety-foot plunge flanked the pier and were the talk of the coast, a must-stop for weekend beach goers with a quarter to burn on the trolley, as well as for the stars of the silent screen arriving in their roadsters and limos. Cecil B. DeMille parted the waters in his first filming of the *Ten Commandments* here, as sightseers plied the beach walk on miniature wicker cars powered by electric motors. A giant roller coaster two blocks long towered over all, and celebrities popped into town aboard their private planes, which landed at the Seal Beach Airport, famous for its Airport Club twenty-four-hour casino. Stop by Clancy's Irish Bar on Main Street today and ask one of our longest-lived natives, T-Bone, about it, how he used to earn tips as a kid chocking the wheels of the stars' planes and wiping the motor oil off their windshields in exchange for rides. He loved the old Seal Beach, the splendid pier and the rickety houses and the air of danger, and he decries the "do-gooders" who, with a firm assist from Prohibition and the Great Depression, ground Seal Beach's incarnation as Sin City into dust. The demise of the Red Cars finished the job. Now the old airport is long gone, and the coaster, and the giant Quonset hut with all-night poker inside is just a skeletal foundation by First Street. T-Bone can't afford to live here anymore—he's in landlocked Westminster down the road.

Except for the sky-high cost of its real estate, the town has marched in the opposite direction from its sister beach cities, becoming smaller, quainter, more family oriented over time. Accidents of geography and government have conspired to accomplish this. Bounded on the south by the ocean, the west by the San Gabriel, and the east by the Seal Beach Naval Weapons Station, much of which is now a nature preserve, Seal Beach has almost no room to grow. Some briefly wise city council in the distant past decided to forbid most apartment buildings and duplexes, and so Old Town has remained pristine and stable, a family zone. Except for new commercial development pushing inland past the 405 Freeway, out past Leisure World and the Boeing facility where moon rockets were once constructed and secret spy satellites are now designed, development has been essentially frozen here since the sixties.

⟿⟿

When I returned to City Hall a few days later to pay my five bucks for *A Story of Seal Beach*, Joanne had some old photo albums waiting for me. A newspaper ad from 1913 stuffed into the front of one caught my attention. It urged L.A. residents to take the train to Seal Beach and to buy a lot for five hundred fifty dollars (only ten percent down!), so that they, too, could enjoy the city that "has no winter and knows no summer . . . growing like a weed and sturdy as an oak." The vision, then, was for Seal Beach to become the biggest, brightest, trendiest coastal city this side of the Bay Area. That vision flourished, briefly, then failed, thankfully, but ninety-one years later it is being resurrected.

The city is hard up for cash—there are million-dollar homes, but no money to pick up beach litter or to keep City Hall open a full five days—and so the push for progress, to grow like a weed, long dormant, is rearing up. One of the last undeveloped pieces of land in town, the old Hellman Ranch next to the "Hill" neighborhood above PCH, is now being graded for new homes, the city allowing an ancient Indian burial ground and wetland to be despoiled in its haste to expand the tax base. The most abominable parts of the project—the hundreds of homes, the golf course, the horrendous traffic problems—were long ago killed by public outcry, and Native American monitors now safeguard the artifacts and burial mounds. Only sixty-four houses remain on the drawing board, along with a restored wetland and a nature preserve to keep safe the legion of foxes and waterfowl and coyotes who live there, not to mention the street-savvy skunks who prowl the neighborhood to scrounge cat food and show my wolfhound who's boss. Still, the change will be jarring; the wide, desolate flatlands next to the fragrant eucalyptus trees of Gum Grove Park, where people run their dogs and hike along the old cow pasture and horse trails, will be gone.

More ominously, the city council, after thirty years of resistance, finally voted to put parking meters on Main Street, a sign that Seal Beach's unique small-town feel is truly on the auction block. This is one of the last beach communities in SoCal where you don't have to dig for quarters. Protests came so swiftly and in such numbers that a shocked and awed council soon rescinded its meter vote—but we all sense, now, that it's only a matter of time. After all, a cell phone shop has just opened on Main Street, an absurdly out-of-place beachhead for chain stores. The fact that no customers ever seem to enter the shop has not as yet deterred its corporate owners.

And another parcel of land, the last undeveloped piece of beachfront in Old Town, where a red-brick power plant long ago stood by the San Gabriel and provided electricity used to help construct the Hoover Dam, is now being eyed by developers and money-hungry council members who have budgets to balance and who can no longer afford The Seal Beach Way. The neighborhood is up in arms, of course, and may yet prevail, or at least limit the damage, but

I can't help but remember Crystal Cove and its vanished paradise, and just how fragile our dreams and myths truly are, at least the ones that count.

Edward Humes, a journalist and author of seven narrative nonfiction books, received the Pulitzer Prize for his newspaper coverage of the military and a PEN Center USA Award for his groundbreaking book about the children of juvenile court, *No Matter How Loud I Shout*. He spent a year inside California's top public school to research his latest critically acclaimed book, *School of Dreams*, named a Best Book of 2003 by the *Washington Post*. His other works include *Baby E.R.*, *Mean Justice* (a *Los Angeles Times* Best Book of 1999) and the bestseller *Mississippi Mud*.

Humes has written for numerous magazines and newspapers and is presently writer at large for *Los Angeles* magazine.

www.edwardhumes.com.

surfacing

by Matt Warshaw

Sixteen-year-old Jay Moriarity from Santa Cruz was so intent on paddling into his first wave of the day and pushing up into the correct stance—and he nailed it, feet spread wide across the deck of his board, head tucked, weight forward and low—that he didn't at first realize he'd lifted off the water and was now surfing through air, just ahead of the curl, thirty feet above sea level.

Moriarity, as the big-wave expression goes, didn't penetrate. The wave had pulsed and expanded as it rolled over Maverick's reef, passing quickly from canted to vertical to concave, at which point Moriarity should have been two-thirds of the way down the face, driving like a javelin for flat water. But a draft of wind had slipped under the nose of Moriarity's surfboard—and instead here he was, still in his best big-wave crouch, levitating near the wave's apex. Now the nose of his board lifted up and backward onto a near-perfect vertical axis, its brightly airbrushed underbelly exposed and sharply limned in the morning light. The crest hooked forward, and

Moriarity's arms came up and spread out from either side of his board, creating a Maverick's tableau that couldn't be taken as anything other than a kind of crucifixion.

The religious metaphor is an easy one to make—since big-wave surfers themselves so often use spiritual terms to characterize and illustrate their sport—but it makes you wonder how God, or Lono, or any such divine presence, could have decided to flick Jay Moriarity, Maverick's youngest and sweetest surfer, into the abyss. He was Jay, no nickname, friendly, wholesome, and unjaded—as compared to Flea, Ratboy, Skindog, and a few of the other red-hot and moderately profane Santa Cruz surfers known collectively as the Vermin.

❧

The previous evening, at about 9 P.M., halfway through his evening shift in the kitchen at Pleasure Point Pizza in Santa Cruz, Moriarity phoned the National Weather Service for the updated buoy and weather report. For the past few days, he'd been tracking a North Pacific storm, and his eyebrows went up in stages as he discovered that the surf was going to be bigger than he'd thought, and it was due to arrive in just a few hours.

At 5 A.M. the next morning, Moriarity steered his mother's Datsun pickup north on Highway 1 out of Santa Cruz, a pair of ten-foot, eight-inch surfboards stacked diagonally in the truck bed. An hour later he pulled off the highway near Pillar Point Harbor, just a few hundred yards north of the Half Moon Bay city limit. Maverick's wasn't visible, but out past the harbor jetty, Moriarity could see smooth, wide-spaced ribbons of swell moving toward shore. Big for sure. Maybe bigger than he'd ever seen it.

Another two dozen people—surfers from San Francisco,

80

Santa Cruz, Half Moon Bay, and Pacifica, along with a few surf photographers and spectators—also were driving toward Maverick's in
the predawn light. Moriarity parked near the harbor, where he was
going to catch a ride on *Lizzie-Lynn*, a twenty-six-foot fishing boat
hired by one of the photographers. Moriarity jogged toward the dock,
a surfboard under each arm. The weather was dry and brittle, in the
upper 40s, but a steady east wind made it seem colder as Moriarity
stepped aboard *Lizzie-Lynn*. The boat began to pitch and roll as it
cleared the harbor entrance, but it was a short ride, and ten minutes
later *Lizzie-Lynn* pulled into a deepwater channel adjacent to
Maverick's, about seventy-five yards south of the breaking surf.

It was just past 7 A.M. Ten riders were already in the water,
loosely clustered and sitting on their boards, alert but casual as they
watched the ocean and waited. The surf had been relatively calm during the boat's approach. Now, almost on cue, a set of waves shifted
through the water about a half-mile past the surfers—all of whom
snapped to attention like pointers.

Moriarity watched the first wave track across the distant part
of the reef, which served as a kind of anteroom for Maverick's-bound
swells. The wave, shaped like a broad-based pyramid, grew steadily,
then fringed along the crest as it intersected with the group of surfers,
their arms like pinwheels as they clambered up the face and dropped,
safe, down the back slope. No takers. Not even an exploratory side-
long look.

Jay Moriarity stood like a tuning fork on the deck of *Lizzie-
Lynn*, staring, almost vibrating with nervous anticipation, three
words looping through his mind—*huge and perfect, huge and perfect.*
Then a pragmatic thought: *too much wind.*

As he ran down his tactical checklist and got ready to slip
over the edge of *Lizzie-Lynn*, Moriarity watched Evan Slater wheel his

board around and paddle into the second wave of the set. Slater got to his feet smoothly, but the wind flicked him sideways—just like that. He landed midway down the face on the small of his back, skipped once, twice, then disappeared as the tube threw out around him like a giant blown-glass bubble and collapsed. "Oh my God!" someone on the boat yelled. Everyone scanned the wave's white-foaming aftermath until Slater's head popped up about a hundred feet shoreward from where he'd gone down. More wild shrieks of amazement—"That was *insane!*"—voices tinged with nervous relief. *Lizzie-Lynn* had been in the channel less than two minutes.

Moriarity squatted down, unzipped his nylon backpack, and pulled out a full-length hood-to-ankle neoprene wetsuit, black with blue accents, plus a long-sleeve polypropylene undershirt, a pair of wetsuit booties, and a pair of webbed gloves. The ocean temperature was a skin-tightening fifty-two degrees, but with this layered outfit he might stay in the water for hours.

⚮

As Moriarity paddled toward the Maverick's lineup, Half Moon Bay's twelve thousand residents were getting showered and dressed, pouring coffee, reviewing the Monday morning headlines, and glancing outside to take note of the ongoing stretch of temperate weather. Commuters moved onto the highways, driving north to San Francisco, south to San Jose, east to Silicon Valley. Most of Half Moon Bay High's students were still sleeping through their first few hours of Christmas vacation.

What Half Moon Bay locals were not doing was paying any attention to the fact that Moriarity, Slater and the rest were at that moment tilting against waves bigger than anything surfers had ever faced anywhere in the world outside of Hawaii. Maverick's would in the days ahead produce international headlines. It would eventually produce bigger surf. But that morning, December 19, 1994, the huge wind-sculpted waves were changing the big-wave surfing landscape— and doing so in showy, dramatic style.

That it was happening in near-seclusion was partly a matter of geography, as Maverick's is hidden from view behind Pillar Point's silt- and sandstone headland and the adjacent boat harbor breakwater. But Maverick's was also relatively unknown: It had publicly debuted to the surf world just eighteen months earlier, in a six-page Surfer magazine feature story. For two years before that, it had been something of a shared secret among twenty-five or so northern California surfers.

In addition, Half Moon Bay wasn't a hard-core surf town, and never had been. San Francisco, twenty-five miles north, had long occupied a special niche in the surf world—partly due to the incredibly photogenic wave that breaks under the southern span of the Golden Gate Bridge, but more so because of the curious and pleasing fact that surfing could take root and flourish on the perimeter of such a famous, sophisticated urban center. Santa Cruz, meanwhile, fifty-eight miles south of Half Moon Bay, had a strong claim as the world's greatest surf city. High-quality surf breaks are strung together like beads along the Santa Cruz coastline and the near-Homeric scope of local surf history goes back to 1885, when Edward, David and Cupid Kawananakoa, three blue-blooded Hawaiian teenagers attending a local military school, crafted boards for themselves from redwood planks and tested the shorebreak near the San Lorenzo rivermouth—becoming not just the first surfers in Santa Cruz but the first surfers in America. Wetsuit magnate Jack O'Neill opened his first shop here in 1959. Tom Curren, three-time world champion and American surfing icon, opened his 1990 world title run with a contest win at Steamer Lane, Santa Cruz's best-known break. A few years later, Darryl Virostko, Josh Loya, Chris Gallagher, Peter Mel, Kenny Collins, Jay Moriarity and other young Santa Cruz locals had collectively become the hottest regionally connected troupe of surfers in California.

Half Moon Bay wasn't off the surfing map entirely in 1994. Some of the reefs north of town occasionally produced good, powerful waves, and the long crescent-shaped beach south of the harbor was a fallback when the surf was small. Local surf history, though, was thin and mostly unrecorded. Just a few people, for instance, knew the story of Maverick, the white-haired German shepherd who, one winter's day in 1961, tore into the water behind three Half Moon Bay surfers as they paddled out to try the distant waves off Pillar Point. One of the surfers, Alex Matienzo, who lived with Maverick's owner, thought the surf looked too rough for the dog. Matienzo paddled back to the beach, whistled Maverick in, and tied him to the car bumper. The waves ended up being too rough for the surfers as well; they soon returned to the beach without having done much riding, and left Pillar Point alone after that. Because Maverick the dog had obviously gotten the most out of the experience, Matienzo and his friends called the intriguing but vaguely sinister Pillar Point surf break "Maverick's Point"—or just Maverick's.

Surfing and surf culture hadn't yet made any real impression in Half Moon Bay, which by 1994 was known more for its weathered rows of cut-flower greenhouses and its neatly groomed acres of brussels sprouts, broccoli, and artichokes, for the horse stables, the stately Beaux-Arts city hall building, the sublime foothill views along Highway 92, and an elaborate and well-attended annual pumpkin festival appropriate for a city billing itself as "The Pumpkin Capital of the World." Strip malls had gone up near downtown and touristy seafood restaurants and nautical-themed gift shops were clustered by the harbor, but local slow-growth advocates had been masterful at keeping large-scale commercialization at bay. They had shut down all attempts to widen Highway 1 and expand the Half Moon Bay airport. Residents, for the most part, were happy to be at a friendly but distinct remove from San Francisco.

Half Moon Bay, the oldest city in San Mateo County, nonetheless has a long and interesting mercantile connection to the sea. Portuguese whalers, in the late nineteenth century, dragged California grays and humpbacks onto the sandy hook of beach just inside Pillar Point, where they rendered slabs of blubber in enormous iron cook pots. Wooden ships were often gutted on the nearby reefs, some producing horrible scenes of splintered planks and floating corpses, others bringing sudden windfall.

During Prohibition, Half Moon Bay bootleggers filled their customized shallow-hulled boats with cases of Canadian-made scotch, rum, gin, and champagne, darted through the surf at night, and made their prearranged drops in the shadowy coves south of Pillar Point. Federal authorities were for the most part outgeneralled by the bootleggers, but in 1932 a midnight skirmish between a Coast Guard patrol boat and a local rumrunner in high seas off Moss Beach resulted in rifle fire, machine gun fire, cannon fire, a kidnapped government agent, some hypothermic open-ocean swimming, two separate chases and four hundred cases of high-quality booze being tossed overboard.

Big fines and the prospect of serious prison time may have forced bootleggers to run this kind of no-surrender gauntlet. But it must have been fantastic open-ocean sport, too. "You experience a thrill and fear at the same time," big-wave surfing pioneer Buzzy Trent wrote in 1965, in a passage that might apply equally to Prohibition bootleggers and Maverick's surfers. "You hear that crack and thunder, you feel the wet spray . . . you just power through, hoping you won't get the ax. And then if you do make it, you get a wonderful feeling inside."

⌒⫠⌐

Jay Moriarity had a different feeling inside—not so wonderful—as he lifted off the face of his giant wave, spread his arms, and hung like a marionette just ahead of the crest. Thirty feet above the trough, he levitated for a little more than a second. The wind then flipped his board back over the top of the wave, and the curl, distended and grossly thick, pitched forward and blotted Moriarity from view. For a half-beat the wave poured forward, untouched and unmarked. Then Moriarity's surfboard reappeared from the wave's back slope and was swiftly pulled forward "over the falls" into the growing thundercloud of whitewater—a bad sign. Moriarity's board was tethered to his ankle by a fifteen-foot, nearly half-inch-thick urethane leash, and the only way it could have been brought back into play was if Moriarity himself, deep and unseen inside the wave, had been dragged down into Maverick's aptly named Pit.

The wave was now a thirty-foot levee of whitewater, crowned by fifty feet of swirling mist and vapor. Below the surface, energy and mass burst downward, creating a field of vertical-flushing gyratory columns, and Moriarity, trapped inside one of these columns, spun end over end until his back and shoulders were fixed against the ocean floor. He clenched, and a bubble of oxygen rushed past his teeth. Maverick's was a deepwater break, he'd been told; nobody ever hit bottom. The next wave would be overhead in another ten or twelve seconds, and Moriarity wondered if, from this depth, he could get to the surface—to air—before it arrived.

Moriarity pushed off and took a huge, sweeping breast-stroke. He opened his eyes to near-opaque blackness. Four more strokes, five, legs in a flutter kick, exhaling slowly, eyes staring upward, stroke, the light becoming a diffuse gray-green, stroke, throat clamped shut, then one last thrust to break the surface—and he threw his head back, mouth stretched open. He'd been down for just over twenty seconds, but he'd beat the second wave—barely. Two quick breaths, and he hunched over defensively as the whitewater roared over, sending him on another underwater loop, shorter but just as violent. Pinpoints of light were zipping across his field of vision by the time he resurfaced.

Moriarity's breath was deep and ragged. There was no third wave. His respiratory rate eased, and as his eyes refocused, he saw that his surfboard was broken in half: the smaller piece—the tail section—was still attached to his leash; the nose section floated nearby. Evan Slater suddenly appeared, looking concerned. Did he need any help? Moriarity shook his head. No, he'd be okay. He swam over to the front half of his surfboard, hoisted himself on deck, and began slowly paddling back to *Lizzie-Lynn*.

In the late eighties, a surf magazine writer theorized that the essential requirement for big-wave riding is not courage, or daring, or fitness, but a placid imagination. Where an ordinary surfer taking full measure of a wave like Maverick's will lose himself in one of a near-endless number of death-by-misadventure scenarios, the big-wave surfer, fantasy-free, paddles out with some degree of aplomb. And as the untroubled imagination reduces fear and anxiety beforehand, it may also smooth things out afterward. Jay Moriarity, a week later, couldn't do much more than sketch out in the most obvious terms the big-wave vignette—generally described at that point as the worst wipeout, or at least the worst looking wipeout, in surfing history— that soon appeared on the cover of *Surfer* and the front section of the *New York Times Magazine*. "I started to stand up," he told *Surfer*, "and thought, 'This will be a cool wave.' Then the whole thing ledged out and I had time to think, 'Oh, shit. This is not good.'"

But maybe that's unfair. Moriarity's banal reaction may have had less to do with a deficient imagination than with the general inarticulateness of sixteen-year-olds. Or perhaps he was just following the form of big-wave protocol that says, play it down, play it cool.

Either way, there was nothing banal about what Moriarity did for an encore that morning. After tossing the pieces of his broken board onto the deck of *Lizzie-Lynn*, he took a short breather, grabbed his reserve board, ran a bar of sticky wax across the top for traction, and paddled back into the lineup.

Forty-five minutes later he caught another wave, nearly as big as the first one, and made it. In the next five hours he caught eight more waves and made them all.

Matt Warshaw edited *Surfer* magazine in the late 1980s, and has written articles for *Outside*, *The New York Times* and *Esquire*. He's written or edited five surfing books, including *The Encyclopedia of Surfing* (2003) and *Maverick's: The Story of Big-Wave Surfing* (2000).

Warshaw lives in San Francisco.

www.mattwarshaw.com.

bienvenidos a newport beach

by Firoozeh Dumas

When I was eleven years old, my father came home and announced that we would soon be moving to Newport Beach. I had never heard of the place but when I told the news to the kids at school, they all said, "Ooooh! You must be rich!"

Our rental in Whittier had a view of the busy main street that I was never allowed to cross by myself, not that I ever wanted to. From our living room window, we could see the big Kentucky Fried Chicken bucket that was always lit up at night. We could also see the Taco Bell and Wienerschnitzel signs. My mom and I had tried a taco once at Taco Bell and really liked it but we had never tried anything at Wienerschnitzel. We never even learned how to pronounce the name. My parents just called it "The Dog Place." We knew there were no dogs in their food but it just seemed like a risk we weren't willing to take.

Our move to Newport Beach would be our eighth. I had

started out in Abadan, Iran, where for six blissful years I lived in the same house. That was the last time I lived in one place for that long.

I was sick of moving and always being the new kid but I really wasn't very fond of our home in Whittier. The neighbors had two dogs that always pooped on our front lawn and when we had asked them to please not let their dogs do that, they had used some four-letter words. My dad didn't know what the words meant exactly, but sometimes you don't need to know the meaning of words to understand the message.

Our other neighbors had a couple of junk cars on their front lawns that were really ugly. Of course, you can do whatever you want with your lawn but putting rusty junkers with no tires on them is just wrong. I don't know why they even kept them. It's not like they were plants that could one day sprout back to life.

Our new rental in Newport Beach was in a "planned community." All the houses looked alike and were maintained by an "Association." This meant that if you wanted to paint your front door fuchsia, you were out of luck. The exterior of your house and all the lawns belonged to the Association. You could do whatever you wanted with the inside, but the outside had to look like everyone else's. When it was time to repaint the exterior of the homes, the Association would have many meetings and then the members would vote. Would it be painted eggshell, off-white, fawn, or ecru? The Association decided.

There were also rules pertaining to trash. Only standard trashcans with lids were allowed. You could not put out your trash more than twenty-four hours in advance, nor could you leave the empty cans out there once the trash had been emptied. You also had to keep your garage door closed. And no cars were allowed to park overnight on the street and it goes without saying that none were allowed on the lawn. But, then again, there were no junkers in Newport Beach, only Cadillacs and other expensive-looking cars. It's funny how people with expensive cars, those cars you wouldn't mind looking at if the owners actually did park them on your front lawn, those owners always put their cars away at night. The uglier the car, the more the owner is willing to share it with the rest of the world.

There were lots of rules for dog owners. They were asked to clean up after their dogs, and most did, thank goodness! Nothing like having to clean someone's doggie souvenirs to make you want to kiss the hand of responsible dog owners.

We felt like we had landed in heaven. Every day when he came home, my dad said he felt like he was on vacation.

What made it seem like a vacation was the pool. For every dozen streets or so, there was a pool. It came with so many rules that there was a whole pamphlet just about the pool rules. Our landlady had mentioned it to us several times, each time TALKING VERY LOUDLY AND S-L-O-W-L-Y.

We had two pool keys and they cost one hundred dollars each to replace. We never lost ours. Lord knows there was more of a chance of my parents losing me in Fashion Island shopping center than them ever losing those pool keys. My mother kept one key hidden at all times. We attached a Universal Studios key chain to the other one and we always kept it in the top drawer in the kitchen. One time two of my cousin's wife's relatives, Touraj and Jamshid, came over and forgot to put the key back in the drawer. I hated having visitors all the time but that's what happens when you move to Newport Beach. Turns out one of them had left the key in the pocket of his terry cloth bathing suit cover. Hadn't they noticed that no one wore those kinds of cover-ups in Newport Beach? It was bad enough that they wore Speedos, which absolutely no one wore. If you asked a man in Newport Beach, "Would you rather die or wear a Speedo?" the answer was obvious. My cousins wondered why none of the cute Kahleefornia girls paid any attention to them.

The pool hours were 7 A.M. to 10 P.M. No loud music. No glass. No unaccompanied guests. We let Touraj and Jamshid go by themselves since frankly, I would not be caught dead with them. They had so much body hair. It was like the Missing Link and his twin were visiting us and using our pool. No way did I want to claim any relationship to those two. Keep the neighbors guessing, I figured.

Of course, if you wanted to have a party, you had to tell the Association, but we never had a party. Iranians don't have pool parties. We have indoor parties where women wear a lot of jewelry and make-up and the men wear suits and talk to other men. Even if we had a pool party, people would still dress the same. We don't do casual pool attire.

I used that pool more than anybody else did in that entire neighborhood. Sometimes you have to live in a house facing the Kentucky Fried Chicken bucket before you can appreciate a clean pool. Every so often, the neighborhood kids threw the pool furniture into the pool at night and ruined it, and then the Association had to take money from the budget to replace the furniture. My father said this is what happens when a person has never been hungry. I had never been hungry but I had never wanted to throw patio furniture into a pool.

All the streets in our planned community had Spanish names starting with "Vista" meaning "view of" in Spanish. This was really wishful thinking since the homes mainly had views of the other houses that looked just like them. There was Vista Suerte, which means View of Luck. I guess you were lucky to have that view instead of a clunker on the neighbor's lawn. There was Vista del Oro, view of gold. I think that referred to real estate prices. My favorite was Vista Roma, view of Rome. That street overlooked the elementary school parking lot. I don't how you say "elementary school parking lot" in Spanish but I'm sure Roma sounds nicer.

You'd think with all the Spanish names there would be a few people speaking Spanish here and there. Twice a week, the Spanish-speaking gardeners came riding in the back of pickup trucks. They'd mow and blow, trim the hedges, cut overgrown branches and look in the houses whenever they could. Who could blame them? I'd be curious, too. Heck, if I were one of the gardeners, I'd bring binoculars.

A couple times a year, the Mexican gardeners would replant the flowers. Corner houses always had a semi-circle of flowers in front of their lawns. The Association decided what to plant. You never saw old flowers in Newport Beach; they were always replaced before they got old. The old people in Newport Beach didn't look so old either. They were always exercising. You'd go to the grocery store and see everyone in tennis clothes. "They're always half naked," my parents used to say.

We didn't look like anybody in our neighborhood. We looked like the gardeners. I think the gardeners knew that too because they always looked at me kind of funny. It was like they wanted to know how I got *in* the house.

Every once in while, one of the neighbors would ask me to please tell that gardener over there that he forgot to trim the hedge on this side. When I'd say I didn't speak Spanish, they were so shocked!

My parents still live in the same house they bought when I was in seventh grade. They have never lost their pool key. The exterior of their house was recently painted Navajo white.

Firoozeh Dumas is the author of *Funny in Farsi*, a *Los Angeles Times* and *San Francisco Chronicle* bestseller and 2004 selection by the "Orange County Reads One Book" program. She was born in Abadan, Iran, and moved to California in the 1970s when her father was an engineer with the National Iranian Oil Company. She wrote her memoir because she wanted her children to know her stories; many middle and high schools and colleges now use her book as part of their curriculums.

Dumas and her French husband, Francois, met at UC Berkeley's International House and live in Northern California with their two children. Their favorite food is sushi.

www.firoozehdumas.com.

cotton candy mirrors

by devorah major

Those adolescent summers seem like such a luxury now; those few years when we were old enough to take the bus by ourselves, and young enough to have only the limited responsibilities of a few daily chores. Summer vacations stretched over three months, and a family vacation rarely took up more than two or three of those weeks. That meant that there were hours upon hours, and days upon days, to fill with adventure. In those years, summers opened each morning, and ended each evening, with the possibility of sitting on porches, watching cars pass, and talking about everything, and talking about nothing. Sometimes the sitting would wear on us, and a football game would be played in the middle of the street, despite nearby parks available in every direction. But some days, pockets full of nickels and dimes, we would cross town to spend the day in our summer school of wonder at Playland at the Beach.

For a one-day tuition of thirty-five cents, with another fifteen cents for a candy bar and a drink, you could spend some time walking around the rides, looking at folks being folks, and then spend hours inside the wooden cavern box that was the Fun House. It wasn't a lot of money, not a lot of money to have, not a lot of money to get. You could find a nickel in the gutter, and collect and return two six-pack soda pop empties at three cents a bottle, and you were in. Education was cheaper, and safer, back in the day.

Most of the time we ate before we left home, or brought along peanut butter and jelly or bologna sandwiches for supplies. Usually there was a nickel left over for a block of pink candied popcorn. You took the 5 McAllister bus, and then walked a block to the painted iron main gate to Playland at the Beach.

Playland had one puny roller coaster that garnered no respect, and only a few, usually false, screams when it crested. There was the inevitable Ferris wheel that took you up higher than the windmills without sails, so that you could see the blue of the Pacific Ocean, the green of Golden Gate Park, and the pale stucco houses of the Richmond district, all laid out around you. There was also an octopus ride that whirled and arched, but never very quickly, and never all that high. The best ride was definitely bumper cars. Before we could get in a car, we would have to watch a few cycles of other drivers, so we could pick a first and second choice in cars, considering color, and maneuverability. When the chain came down we would rush across the slippery floor to secure our vehicle, while a man yelled repeatedly in a tired, crusted voice, "Do not run. Do not run. No running is allowed."

Of course, there were the rows of arcade games. Throw money on a plate, or in a cup, or in a goldfish bowl. Pop balloons, or shoot, ducks or racehorses. And then there was Fascination. The almost always old, and usually only, women, sat on red plastic-covered stools playing Fascination for hours. They would just plunk their dimes on the counter and play, and when they played I never saw the women smile or laugh. I once had a friend who had a mother who would sit, glassy-eyed and staring at the light bulb wall that would light up in bingo lines. One afternoon my friend and I went to say hello to her mother. I think she netted a quarter from the brief between-game exchange; those minutes before her mother returned to staring at the lighting up sequence of lights deciding where winning would next lie.

The electric laughing lady presided over Playland. She stood on a platform at least twenty feet in the air, and seemed as wide as she was tall. With red hair flaming, and striped legs stiff underneath her electronically swaying torso, the laughing clown lady rocked back and forth, high in her rounded glass cage, screeching out her arcade laugh every few minutes. Her cackle was everywhere, except inside the Fun House. It scared small children, irritated adults, and fascinated those in the middle like us. We worked to do imitations, stood around the bottom of the pole mimicking her until we were actually laughing, while she was trapped in endless recorded cackles.

Now, we often had to pass up the rides because we didn't have enough money. We often had to forgo the sugar treats. But the Fun House, the Fun House alone, was reason to make the long cross-city trip. I don't remember ever standing in a long line to get into the Fun House. The place could always fit another child, or another six children, or another class full of children. Oh they made you trickle in, in ones, twos or threes, but only so that you could get full effects of entering this magical playground, of moving into another world.

After paying our money to the ticket person, who occasionally was actually a lover of children who would let you in though a couple of cents short, or encourage you to have a good time, but was, more often, a surly, pudgy faced, short-tempered man or woman who clearly would rather be anywhere else but there, we began our journey with a trek through the hall of mirrors. As soon as we were through the door we were surrounded by mirrors. We hit wall after wall seeking the one passageway that would lead us out of this hallway of ever-changing illusion. Each passageway we thought we saw turned out to be just a reflection of ourselves, and we would find ourselves banging our foreheads, smashing our noses, and slapping our hands against the smooth glass mirrors. After several trips I had memorized the pattern of the first few turns, and could walk with more assurance and not bump into the first three rooms of mirrors, but by the fourth turn my eyes had crossed, and left and right had lost all meaning. I walked slowly, not wanting to walk hand out-stretched like a timid mouse sniffing through the rooms, but also not wanting to bump full force into a mirror wall.

We were surrounded by ourselves in this hallway. The mirrors went on and on and on. You got smaller and smaller and smaller if you tried to count how many mirrors there were reflecting mirrors of yourself, reflecting mirrors of yourself, reflecting mirrors of yourself. The light was muted so that it was hard to see the space formed between true passageway and far wall mirror. Depending on your willingness to take wrong turns and have multiple collisions, it could take you five or thirty minutes to navigate the maze. You crashed, looked, laughed, and turned a corner, bounced again corner-to-corner, until at last you emerged. You found yourself in the main room, where you were assaulted by the whirr of machines, the screams of other children, the cautioning yells of parents, and the smell of air full of sweat and salt.

But you were not *all the way* in the Fun House just because you navigated the hall of mirrors, not at all. After the mirrors there were whirling, headless, iron-framed, cloth-covered cylinders that spun the length of a full wall. The only way forward was to work through, pressed by the wind of their sails, squeezed by the wire in their frames. You had to press through the headless gnomes, taking care not to get caught by their metal torsos that crushed and pinched you as they spun round and round.

After that was the final gauntlet, the floor with air holes. A man sat in a booth across from the entrance and spurted sharp gusts of wind through holes in the floor. Sometimes it was not too harsh and it tickled, most times it was pointed full force and it stung. It was strong and seemed arbitrary where it came up and where it did not. We would watch others run through trying to judge which holes had recently whistled, and which had not. Then we would run across the polished wood floor as fast as we could. Sometimes one or more of us made the error of wearing a skirt and paid another fee on the final entrance to the cavern-like room. The harsh air blew up the wide cotton skirts, the ones with hems that ended mid-calf and fell in folds around our hips. There was no way to avoid every single hole that was carved into the floor. It was impossible to know from where the next gust would come. So we rushed in a zigzag pattern, leaning over, holding down dresses, through the gauntlet of air hoses that would reveal young thighs, and give hints of white underpants. But after that, finally, we were in a wooden cavern full of laughter, screams, hundreds of chances to take, and hundreds of lessons to learn.

To the left was a smooth silver disk wide enough to hold two dozen children, more if some were really small, and the adult at the controls wasn't paying too much attention. First we would all pile onto the disk, racing for the middle, which yielded the longest ride to the strongest of our crew. When we were all on, holding on to each other, holding on to our knees, pressed into the coldness of the steel; when we were all on, the man on the side would pull a gear and the disc would begin to spin. It would become a flying saucer that never quite left the ground. Before the second spin was completed, before the people watching turned to blurs and your own squeals warbled against your eardrums, some children began to fly off the ride, while others—Keds, Converses or PF Flyers dug into the metal, fingers gripping the edge—tried to be the last ones on the disk, tried to stay on as long as possible before sliding to the edge, and then rolling laughing across the floor. It never was a question of how the ride ended. Always it was you sliding on your back, or on your belly, or on your side, maybe pulled by another, maybe holding onto a friend's shirttail. Whatever technique you picked, sooner or later you too would be hurled off the disk. Getting spun off was taken for granted. The point was how long you lasted in the spin, and how quickly you got back on the ride for another try.

From there it was a short run to the barrel ride. The barrel was at least eight feet in diameter. Several children could walk or skip or jump through it end to end, while it turned on its side speeding up, and then slowing. Some children walked to the middle and then stayed holding onto the sides. Some ran, legs spread wide trying not to lose their footing, as they stepped against the roll crossing wooden slats. Some children became trapped and couldn't get out. They gave up and finally resorted to crawling to escape the barrel. Some got completely stuck. If they got too scared and started crying, or even just whining, despite our shouts of encouragement or derision, the man who ran the ride would stop the barrel and let them off. The child would be harshly teased if he or she was too old to be pulling that stuff, or gently consoled if it was youngster trying to have heart like their older brother or sister.

After a few runs through the barrel you were ready for the super slide. To go on this wooden slide you had to take off your shoes and then climb three flights of stairs, usually slowly because there was always a line for this diversion. At the top of the slide you picked up a piece of burlap. While you stood waiting for your turn, the whole Fun House spread out beneath you. People were so much smaller at the top, and you could see how long the slide really was. But there was no backing down. Rarely would a child refuse to go, and risk facing the comments of each child they had to pass while climbing back down the stairs. When your turn finally came, you sat on the burlap, so your skin on your legs wouldn't burn if you were wearing shorts, or the skin on the palms of your hands, if you put them at your sides in a hopeless attempt at controlling the speed of descent. Then with a deep breath, down you shot, gulping air, making wind fly all around you, feeling the heat of the wood beneath you. You rushed down three long hills of thickly lacquered, shiny wood. When you reached the bottom, still carrying the wind trapped in your lungs, still unable to speak, you got up, and went to the back of the line, so you could climb up those stairs and do it all over again.

To quiet ourselves, and take a break from the climbing, yelling, falling, jumping and screaming, we would clamber up a narrow set of stairs on one side or the other of the cavernous Fun House. There, on a thin mezzanine, was a balcony of distorting mirrors. In these mirrors we became monsters, we became clowns, we were lengthened, flattened, rounded. Our eyes grew as we made faces, pushed out our lips and pulled on our ears, distorting the image more completely, turning ourselves into alien beings, into insects, into comedians. I would stand in front of these mirrors and try to correct the image, try to see myself as I really was. It was a silly game, pretending that a Fun House mirror was a real mirror. It was a foolish pretense making believe that by squinting or broadening my eyes, the image reflected would somehow be closer to the truth. Not that mirrors were entirely deceptive, it was, after all, myself that I saw, or at least a form of myself, in those mirrors.

And those quiet times in the mirrors showed a lot. Although they tore down the Fun House, the mirrors still exist. I went on seeing them in my television set, in the billboards posted around town, in music video and CDs telling me and my children lies about ourselves, distorting our history. I never stopped seeing those mirrors that made some features larger, while diminishing others, that made us seem squashed and wide, or spindling tall, but always made us look weak and wavy.

I learned from the mirrors at the beginning of the Fun House, to the mirrors at the end not to take reflections too seriously as the real thing. In fact, I don't even look at regular mirrors too often these days, now knowing that the right lighting can hide any number of sins, or reveal every detail of abuses. I've learned to use the eyes of others as my mirrors. But only those people whose eyes are clear and shine with laughter and love.

Still it was the Fun House where I first learned about mirrors. It was in the Fun House that I learned about holding on and letting go. Summer was time of education and character building and though there was time to waste, there was not too much time, because fall was always just around the corner. And with the heat of September came public school, with its calling forth of names and dates, and endless teacher-echoes of "Because I said so" and "Maybe it doesn't make sense. Nevertheless, those are the rules" and "You have to learn it because it's a requirement." But it was the summer learning, the lessons on when to jump and when to stay still, when to show courage even when you didn't have it, when to use a surprise attack to throw off your opponent—it was those classes that helped us in ways we didn't expect, so that we could surmount the trials that faced us in, and out, of the official educational institutions of our childhood.

---

devorah major became the third Poet Laureate in San Francisco in 2002. Her poetry books include *street smarts* and *where river meets ocean*. She also has two novels, *An Open Weave* and *Brown Glass Windows*. Her poems, short stories and essays are available in a number of magazines and anthologies. She has taught poetry and creative writing as community artist-in-residence and college lecturer for more than twenty years.

major also publishes, records and performs with Opal Palmer Adisa in the performance poetry group Daughters of Yam (www.daughtersofyam.com). She was born and raised in California.

berkeley

by Michael Chabon

W here passion is married to intelligence, you may find genius, neurosis, madness or rapture. None of these is really an unfamiliar presence in the tree-lined streets of Berkeley, California. For a city of one hundred thousand people— toss in another thirty thousand to account for the transient population of the University—we have more than our share of geniuses. The town, to be honest, is lousy with them. Folklorists, chefs, tattoo artists, yogis, guitarists, biologists of the housefly, GUI theorists, modern masters of algebra, Greil Marcus: we have geniuses in every field and discipline. As for neurosis, you can pretty much start at my house and work your way outward in any direction. Obsession, fixation, phobia, hypochondriasis, self-flagellation, compulsive confession of weakness and wrongdoing, repetition mania, chronic recrimination and second-guessing—from parents of toddlers, to fanatical collectors of wax recordings by Turkish klezmer bands of the 1920s, to non-eaters of anything white or which respires, to that august tribunal of collective neurosis, the Berkeley City Council: if neuroses were swimming pools one might, like Cheever's swimmer, steer a course from my house to the city limits and never touch dry land. Madness: a painful thing, which it does not do to romanticize. But it seems to me that among the many sad and homeless people who haunt Berkeley one finds an unusually high number of poets, sages, secret Napoleons and old-fashioned prophets of doom. The mentally ill citizens of Berkeley read, as they kill a winter afternoon in the warmth of the public library; they generate theories, which they will share; they sell their collected works out of a canvas tote bag. As for rapture, it is harder to observe firsthand, and is furthermore something that people, even people in Berkeley, do not necessarily care to discuss. But Berkeley is rich with good places to be rapt: at the eyepiece of an electron microscope or a cloud chamber, at a table at Chez Panisse, in a yoga room, under a pair of headphones at Amoeba Records, in Tilden Park, in the great disorderly labyrinth of Serendipity Books, on the dance floor at Ashkenaz while the ouds jangle and the pipes skirl, in a seat at the Pacific Film Archive watching Kwaidan (Japan, 1965). I'd be willing to bet that, pound for pound, Berkeley is the most enraptured city in America on a daily basis.

If that statement has the ring of boosterism, then permit me to clarify my feelings on the subject of my adopted home: this town drives me crazy. Nowhere else in America are so many people obliged to suffer more inconvenience for the common good. Nowhere else is the individual encumbered with a greater burden of shame and communal disapproval for having intruded, however innocently, on the sensibilities of another. Berkeley's streets, though a rational nineteenth-century grid underlies them, are a speed-busting tangle of artificial dead ends, obligatory left turns and deliberately tortuous obstacle-course barriers known as chicanes, put in place to protect children—who are never (God forbid!) sent to play outside. Municipal ordinances intended to protect the nobility of labor in Berkeley's attractive old industrial district steadfastly prevent new-economy businesses from taking over the aging brick-and-steel structures—leaving them empty cenotaphs to the vanished noble laborer of other days. People in the grocery store, meanwhile, have the full weight of Berkeley society behind them as they take it upon themselves to scold you for exposing your child to known allergens or imposing on her your own indisputably negative view of the universe. Passersby feel empowered—indeed, they feel duty-bound—to criticize your parking technique, your failure to sort your recycling into brown paper and white, your resource-hogging four-wheel-drive vehicle, your use of a pinch-collar to keep your dog from straining at the leash.

When Berkeley does not feel like some kind of vast exercise in collective dystopia—a kind of left-wing Plymouth Plantation in which a man may be pilloried for over-illuminating his house at Christmastime—then paradoxically it often feels like a place filled with people incapable of feeling or acting in concert with each other. It is a city of potterers and amateur divines, of people so intent on cultivating their own gardens, researching their own theories, following their own bliss, marching to their own drummers and dancing to the tinkling of their own finger-cymbals that they take no notice of one another at all, or would certainly prefer not to, if it could somehow be arranged. People keep chickens, in Berkeley—there are two very loud henhouses within a block of my house. There may be no act more essentially Berkeley than deciding that the rich flavor and healthfulness, the simple, forgotten pleasure, of fresh eggs in the morning outweighs the unreasonable attachment of one's immediate neighbors to getting a good night's sleep.

The result, perhaps inevitable, of this paralysis of good intentions, this ongoing, floating opera of public disapproval and the coming into conflict of competing visions of the path to personal bliss, is a populace inclined to kvetching and to the wearing of the default Berkeley facial expression, the suspicious frown. Bliss is, after all, so near at hand; the perfect egg, a good night's sleep, reconciliation with one's mother or the Palestinians, a theory to account for the surprising lack of dark matter in the universe, a radio station that does not merely parrot the lies of government flaks and corporate media outlets—such things can often feel so eminently possible here, given the intelligence and the passion of the citizens. And yet they continue to elude us. Who is responsible? Is it us? Is it you? What are you doing, there, anyway? Don't you know the recycling truck won't take aluminum foil?

So much for boosterism. And yet I declare, unreservedly and with all my heart, that I love Berkeley, California. I can't imagine living happily anywhere else. And all of the things that drive me crazy are the very things that make this town worth knowing, worth putting up with, worth loving and working to preserve.

Part of the charm of Berkeley lies in her setting: the shimmer and eucalyptus sting of the hills on a dusty summer afternoon, hills whose rocky bones jut through the skin of Berkeley in odd out-croppings like Indian Rock; the morning fogs of the flatlands along the bay, with their smell of mud and their magically vanishing glimpses of Alcatraz and towers of San Francisco. But I have lived in places, from the Puget Sound to the Hudson Valley, from Laguna Beach to Key West, that rivaled if not surpassed Berkeley in spectacular weather, thrilling vistas and variety of terrain. Not, perhaps, all at the same time, but to greater extremes of beauty. And yet a city with a beautiful site is about as reliably interesting as a person with a beautiful face, and just about as likely to have been spoiled.

Laid atop her remarkable setting between hills and bay, less consistently fine but at its best no less charming, is the built environment of Berkeley. The town, though laid out in the 1880s, boomed in the aftermath of the 1906 earthquake and fire, when it was settled by refugees from San Francisco, fleeing hither under the mistaken impression that the jutting rock ribs of Berkeley's hills would be proof against temblors. The town grew explosively, to its borders, in the twenty years that followed, and as a result the architecture, especially that of her houses, has a pleasing uniformity of variation, with styles ranging from Prairie school to Craftsman to the various flavors of Spanish. There is even a local style—I live in an exemplar, built in 1907—called the Berkeley Brown Shingle, which combines elements of the Craftsman and the Stick: overhanging eaves, square-pillared porches, elaborate mullions and built-in cabinetry, the whole enveloped in a rustic skin of the eponymous cedar or redwood shakes. It's a sober style, at least in conception, boxy and grave and appropriately professorial, and yet after decades of benign neglect and dreaminess and the ministrations of an unstintingly benevolent climate, the houses tend to be wildly overgrown with rose vines, wisteria, jasmine, trumpetvine and outfitted top and sides with unlikely modifications: Zen dormers, orgone porches, Lemurian observatories. Certain of her streets offer endless instruction in the rich and surprising expressiveness of brown, houses the color of brown beer, of brown bread, of tobacco, a dog's eyes, a fallen leaf, an old upright piano. The harmoniousness of Berkeley's streets and houses is far from perfect—there are tons of hideous concrete-and-aluminum dingbat monstrosities, in particular around the university, and downtown is a hodgepodge of doughty old California commercial structures, used car lots and a few truly lamentable late-sixties office towers. But even the most down-at-heel and ill-used streets offer a promise of green shade in the summertime, and many neighborhoods are densely populated by trees, grand old plantations of maple and oak, long rows of ornamental plums that blossom in the winter, persimmon trees, Meyer lemon trees, palm trees and fig trees, monkey puzzles and Norfolk island pines, redwoods and Monterey pines nearly a hundred years old. One of the remarkable things about Berkeley is that, in spite of its decided inferiority to its great neighbor across the Bay in clout, preeminence, population, notoriety and fame, it has never seemed to dwell in San Francisco's shadow (unlike poor old Oakland down the road). I believe that this may be in part due to the fact that when it comes to trees—a necessary component, in my view, of the greatness of a city—the Colossus of the West can't hold a candle to Berkeley.

But houses and tree plantations, like hills and foggy mudflats, are no reliable guarantors of the excellence of a place to live. That elusive quality always lies, ultimately, in the citizenry; in one's neighbors. And it is ultimately the people of Berkeley—those same irritating frowners and scolders, those very neurotic geniuses and rapt madwomen—who make this place, who ring an endless series of variations on its great theme of personal and communal exploration, and who, above all, fight tooth and nail to hang on to what they love about it.

If there were a hundred good small cities in America fifty years ago—towns built to suit the people who settled them, according to their tastes, aspirations and the sovereign peculiarities of landscape and weather—today there are no more than twenty-five. In ten years, as the inexorable lattice of sprawl replicates and proliferates, and the downtowns become malls, and the malls downtowns, and the rich syllabary of mercantile America is reduced to a simple alphabet composed of a Blockbuster, a Target, a Starbucks, a Barnes and Noble, a Gap and a T.G.I. Friday's, and California herself is drowned in a sea of red-tile roofs from San Ysidro to Yreka, there may be fewer than ten. When the end finally comes, I believe that Berkeley will be the last town in America with the ingrained perversity to hold onto its idea of itself. This is a town—on the edge of the country, on the edge of the twenty-first century, on the edge of subducting plates and racial divides and an immense sea of corporate homogeneity—where you can still sign for your groceries at the store around the corner. A Berkeley grocer is a man who preserves such an archaic custom not in spite of the fact but exactly because it's an outmoded and cumbersome way of running a business.

It's in the quirky, small businesses of Berkeley, in fact, places like the old soda fountain in the Elmwood Pharmacy, Alkebulan Books (specializing in books on the African diaspora), d.b.a. Brown

Records (just on the Oakland side of the city limits) or the Sound Well (used and vintage hi-fi and stereo equipment) that the tensions of Berkeley living, the competing claims on the heart of a Berkeleyite to follow one's bliss but at the same time to reach a hand out into the void and feel another set of fingers taking hold of one's own, are resolved. These are not merely retail establishments, poor cousins of Rite-Aid, Borders, Sam Goody's and Circuit City. They are shrines to the classic Berkeley impulse to latch on to something tiny but crucial—the warm sound provided by vacuum-tube amplifiers, the mid-sixties sides of Ornette Coleman, the African roots of Jesus Christ and his teachings or a perfectly constructed Black-and-White (with an extra three inches in the steel blender cup)—and pursue it with a mounting sense of self-discovery. And yet they are also, accidentally but fundamentally, gathering places; they all have counters at which the lonely amateur of Coleman or Marantz, the student of Martin Bernal can pull up a stool and find him- or herself in the company of sympathetic minds. Berkeley is richer than any place I've ever lived in these non-alcoholic taverns of the soul, these unofficial clubhouses of the oddball and outré. And it seems as if every year another one pops up, at the bottom of Solano Avenue, in a faded brick stretch of San Pablo Avenue, unfranchisable, inexplicable except as a doorway to fulfillment and fellowship. A business that would never thrive anywhere else, patronized by people who would never thrive anywhere else, in a city that lives and dies on the passion and intelligence, the madness and rapture, of its citizens.

Michael Chabon is the author of two short-story collections and four novels, including *The Mysteries of Pittsburgh*, *Wonder Boys* and *The Amazing Adventures of Kavalier & Clay*. His most recent book is the young adult novel *Summerland*. Chabon's work has appeared in such magazines as *The New Yorker*, *Harper's*, *GQ*, *Esquire* and *Playboy* and in a number of anthologies, among them *The O. Henry Prize Stories* and *Best American Short Stories*.

In 2001, Chabon won the Pulitzer Prize for fiction for his novel *The Amazing Adventures of Kavalier & Clay*. He lives in Berkeley with his wife, Ayelet Waldman, also a novelist, and their children.

www.michaelchabon.com.

california honky-tonk

by Kathi Kamen Goldmark

Y ou'd think he might have mentioned it was a biker bar. To us, four young folksingers who'd teamed up on a cute half-hour set as an assignment for our Intermediate Performance Workshop, it felt like the big time—a club owner had come backstage and offered us our very first real bar gig down in San Pedro. It never occurred to us to ask if there would be bikers.

The thing is, we weren't exactly a band. Well, we thought we were. But we didn't have a rhythm section—who knew you even needed a rhythm section?—and we didn't have a PA, or a manager, or any of the other stuff bands are supposed to have, like four hours' worth of material. We did have some nice guitars, some sweet vocal harmonies, and a couple of folkie performances under our belts. And we had outfits. Thanks to my trusty glue gun, rhinestone-studded satin shirts were imminent; thanks to my brand-new credit card, so were bona fide cowboy hats that had most certainly never been anywhere near a cow.

Realizing that we needed to beef up our set list, we decided some research was in order, so Lonesome Ed was dispatched on a stealth mission. He sat quietly in a corner of the bar, a classy joint called Sinbad's Saloon, and carefully noted every song the regulars played on the jukebox. The clear front-runner, played over a dozen times that evening, was "Why Don't We Get Drunk and Screw?" by Jimmy Buffett. Lonesome Ed copied the lyrics onto a cocktail napkin, and drove on home.

The next few days were a blur of rehearsals that went late into the night, poring through songbooks, scratching up our records trying to get down lyrics, rhinestone studding, more rehearsing, more rhinestone studding. We added thirty songs to our repertoire, all with unique and interesting three and four-part harmonies. We had tense discussions about who would sing which song, who would take a solo here or there. As lead singer, it was my job to learn "Why Don't We Get Drunk and Screw?" and I managed a competent rendition. Along with our lovely, intricate vocal arrangements of "San Antonio Rose" and "Ripple" it would work just fine. Who cared if we'd lost sleep, missed work, maxed out our MasterCards? It was worth it for our big gig. I bought a tambourine and decorated it with rhinestones and ribbons. By Friday night, we were ready for our first real country-western show in a California honky-tonk.

In Lonesome Ed's van, on the way to the gig, we suddenly remembered that our band had no name. As luck would have it, the thought occurred to us as we were passing a place called the El Rancho Motel.

"That's it!" cried Reverend Big Chris, our lead guitarist, a rugby player who'd earned his nickname by accepting ordination in lieu of cash at a recent church gig—he's performing wedding ceremonies to this day, but that's another story.

"Huh?" I'd been too busy chasing AWOL rhinestones under

the dashboard to look up.

"El Rancho Motel! It's a perfect name for our band. You know, 'third rate romance, low-rent rendezvous'"—as he sang the chorus of the Amazing Rhythm Aces song we'd chosen to kick off our first set. So El Rancho Motel we became.

The club owner looked a little surprised when we rolled in wearing eighty pounds of spangles and carrying acoustic guitar cases, with no drummer, backline, or PA. But he rigged up a minimal sound system for us, and we got ready to play.

The club was slowly filling up with regulars and one of them—a woman with the biggest hair, tightest pants, and pointiest cleavage I'd ever seen—took an immediate interest in our little huddle on the bandstand. She grabbed my hand and dragged me into the ladies room for an instant makeover. Five minutes later, wearing nine or ten extra pounds of makeup and my new friend Ginny's lace camisole under my now-unbuttoned blouse, I was ready. Move over Patsy, move over Dolly, Linda, and Emmylou. I had glitter in my hair and I was ready to sing.

But really, there was no way for me to be ready for what happened next, when an entire motorcycle gang came roaring into the parking lot on their Harleys for their regular Friday night meeting, led by a four-hundred-pound shaved-headed bruiser named Lobo. About then it dawned on us that all our intricate four-part vocal arrangements, and all our carefully rehearsed mandolin-guitar counterpoints were about as appropriate as tits on a bull. The bikers were yelling for Lynyrd Skynrd and the Allman Brothers; we were giving them Geoff and Maria Muldaur, only wimpier. They wanted to drink and dance and get laid; our rhythm section was a beribboned tambourine.

And then Lonesome Ed remembered our ace in the hole, our secret weapon—the most-requested tune on the Sinbad's Saloon jukebox, "Why Don't We Get Drunk and Screw?" He slipped me the rumpled cocktail napkin with the lyrics, and I started the song. The crowd hushed just a bit, a few people started to sing along, a few more danced. I got more confident, louder and saucier. It was finally working—we were winning them over at last. And then out of nowhere, looming over the bandstand was Lobo. All four hundred, shaved-headed pounds of scary bellowing biker yelling, "I'm drunk, let's screw!" into my microphone, as he picked me up in one enormous muscled arm and started walking toward the door.

⌒╫⌐

I've thought of that night thirty years ago many times, while gradually figuring out what it takes to please a honky-tonk crowd (here's a hint: no one cares about the rhinestones on your tambourine), how to find that magical mix of musicians that makes a band sound right, why a rhythm section is a good thing, and a solid groove even better, and how to figure out what a crowd wants—and give it to them. I've had some highs to rival my Sinbad's low: nights when the band was so tight, the crowd so with us, that it felt like magic; and one night in particular, when I'd asked a bunch of authors who all wished they were rock stars to join me onstage for a benefit gig at a book convention. Surprisingly, they did. Even more surprisingly, the night was an incredible success—partly, I think, because the Rock Bottom Remainders chose to throw our party not in a hotel ballroom, as suggested, but in a honky-tonk: the Cowboy Boogie in Anaheim, California.

I've been in many bands since Sinbad's Saloon, and I've played in clubs with names every bit as picturesque, all over California: The Soundtrack in San Francisco, where the owner would

complain if we didn't draw a crowd, then complain (when we responded by getting all our friends to come) that there were too many
"strangers" in her bar; the Sundowner in Benicia, where the best part
was staying after the gig to have biscuits and gravy for breakfast, getting home just before sunrise; the Hopland Brewery, where I had to
miss a gig because my nine-month-old son, not having a fake ID, was-
n't allowed to snooze in his babysitter's arms in the backroom; one
club where we actually played on top of the bar (it was clear that
everyone was looking up your skirt the whole time); and another
where a car drove clear through the wall and the band kept playing.

My favorite, the one that became my band's home base in
later years, was DeMarco's 23 Club in Brisbane. In its heyday, the
club hosted some country music greats, and proudly displayed their
photos on the wall. Owner Lil DeMarco became a dear friend—she'd
wink her approval from her regular bar stool when I sang a song she
liked; she never turned my music-loving son away even though at age
ten he still didn't have the fake ID thing together. Lil took special care
to see that her favorite female patrons and performers were comfort-
able and safe, a fact that was mentioned over and over again at her
funeral a few years ago. Since then, the club has gone through a few
transformations. It spent a brief period pretending to be a Goth club,
and is now leased to a Russian restaurateur. But the photos are still
up on the wall, the bartender still remembers the night a guy got shot
at a Ray Price show; there's sometimes a rockabilly show if you hit it
on the right night—the honky-tonk shines through at DeMarco's,
and I hope it always will.

As for Sinbad's Saloon, who knows? Though El Rancho
Motel stayed together for a while, we never got another gig there.
After I'd been "picked up" by Lobo, my new best friend Ginny wig-
gled over and distracted him with her amazing cone-shaped cleavage

until he literally dropped me—in the middle of the dance floor. I dust-ed myself off and sang some more hippie harmonies for folks who real-ly wanted to dance to hard rock. We got paid, packed up our gear, and went home.

The only real injury I sustained was a black-and-blue thigh, not from being dropped on my butt by a four hundred-pound biker, but from hitting myself, over and over again in the same spot, with a rhinestone-studded tambourine. It was a little embarrassing at the time, and I never told anyone about my bruised leg—or my bruised ego. But bruises heal, and sometimes even turn into good stories. I have a feeling that if Lil DeMarco heard this one, she'd have loved it.

Kathi Kamen Goldmark is the author of *And My Shoes Keep Walking Back to You*, a novel published by Chronicle Books in 2002. She is the co-author of *The Great Rock & Roll Joke Book* and *Mid-Life Confidential: The Rock Bottom Remainders Tour America with Three Chords and an Attitude*.

Goldmark also is the founder of the all-author rock band The Rock Bottom Remainders; president and janitor of Don't Quit Your Day Job Records; and producer of the coast-to-coast radio show "West Coast Live." She lives in San Francisco.

www.dqydj.com.

909

by Percival Everett

909 is a little like the name Bob. It's the same forwards and backwards. In fact, inverted, 909 is 'Bob', or at least 'bob'. There's a friendly ring to Bob, a familiarity. You don't call him Robert, you call him Bob. Bob is your plumber, your cable installer, your mechanic. In my case, my farrier. Bob is blue-collar, sweaty, down-to-earth. And that's how 213, 310, 714, 323 and 626 see 909. This is where I live, out in Riverside County about halfway to Palm Springs in desert hills known as the Badlands.

People in Los Angeles fight over area codes. They care what their codes are. I understand that the best one to have is 310 or maybe 213. But out here we don't care. We live in towns called Banning and Temecula and Cabazon, separated not by an avenue, but by mountains or expanses of desert. We used to be orange groves and wheat fields, horse and cattle ranches. Now, we're tracts of affordable houses for people with too many children and jobs for people like Bob. We are known for meth labs and prisons and brutal summers and the occasional cougar wandering through town. Years ago the Mission Inn was the place where movie stars went to do whatever they later came to do in Palm Springs. Then someone discovered Palm Springs and so we became the space between Los Angeles and Palm Springs, the distance that made Palm Springs a getaway. The Mission Inn closed and remained closed for a long time and is now reopened. It is a kind of marker of what was, a luxury hotel in a place where no one comes. It's a nice hotel—beautiful, mission style and quaint and a place that no doubt sees its share of weddings and banquets. I'm sure it's where the president might stay during an election year visit. There is a chair in the lobby there made especially for William Taft, extra wide and the story goes that he was, rightly, insulted by it. That might be the story of Riverside. Trying to fit in with the big boys by accommodating their oversized posteriors.

Out here, a lot of us have land and on that land we have horses. We're horsey out here. That's how we say it. We say, "This is a horsey area." And we have signs that depict basketball-headed silhouette humans seated on silhouette horses. That means go slow. We have feed stores and tack shops and desert, a really beautiful desert. It's the desert that has me here in 909.

Technically, the Badlands is chaparral. The hills are filled with sage, wild mustard, fiddleheads and live oaks. Bobcats, meadowlarks, geckos, horned lizards, red tailed hawks, kestrels, coach whip snakes, king snakes, gopher snakes. Rattlesnakes and coyotes. We don't see rain for seven months of the year and when we do we often flood. In the spring, the hills are green. They are layered and gorgeous. This is in contrast to the rest of the year when the hills are brown and ochre and layered and gorgeous. From my place I can see ten-thousand-foot Mount San Jacinto, sometimes topped with snow, most times not and occasionally hidden from view by some kind of inversion or smog. It is through all of this that I ride my mule. I can ride deep into the hills and I don't know there's anyone within a hundred miles of me. The trails are rough, steep, and sometimes a yard wide with long drops on either side. Of course this is why I'm alone back here.

Out here in 909, I saddle my mule while my neighbor to the north lunges a beautiful paint horse. I can hear the faint music of her radio. It's some kind of country music, not the same concertina music that wafted through the pastures from another house last night. My mule doesn't care about the activity. He stands with his big head low and awaits the saddle. It's August and the temperature will rise to one hundred eight. It's perhaps ninety-five right now at nine-thirty. If I don't ride now, I probably won't today. I'm using my cavalry saddle because it's cooler for the animal, though hard on my backside, and because I just think it's cool. I tighten the cinch and I listen. I want to know if there are any illegal dirt bikers out in the hills or whether someone is shooting at quail or cans or each other. Monk, that's my mule's name, and I climb the hill on the east side of the ranch and cross over onto a vast stretch of empty county and state land.

Before I head up, I swing south and around a crater that was caused by an exploded automobile. We speculate that car thieves destroyed the thing out here because it's so far away from anyone (except us). The explosion caused a brush fire that got squashed pretty quickly by firefighters, but it left a blackened and cleared area. I'm taking this opportunity to teach Monk to deal with strange and unfamiliar terrain. He doesn't like it. He dances off the charred ground and looks back at me, as if to ask, "Why would someone do this in our hills?" I tell him I don't know and guide him closer to a burned shrub and he sniffs it. I wonder what would have happened if I had come upon the criminals in mid-act? It sounds scary and all my city friends think of 909 as the wild outback, but I'm less likely to have a run-in with a crook out here than in 213.

Monk and I travel on, up and down and farther into the hills, past where I found the coyote den last year, past where Monk once shied from a balloon caught in a tree; there was an eye painted on it. We pause to watch a rattler cross the trail. Snakes don't bother Monk and I'm five feet off the ground, so I'm not bothered either. We watch him slither down the slope and into the high grass. There is no shade to speak of out here; the trees grow to nine or ten feet only in the bottoms of narrow arroyos that are so full of brush there is no getting close. We pop brush and make our way to a high place. The cracking of the dead weeds and shrubs is frightening. This stuff feels like it could ignite spontaneously. At the top I look down over the Moreno Valley, aptly named for this time of year, brown valley. Lake Perris is south. Also to the south is Mystic Lake, not a lake at all, but a huge wet spot that has diminished every year of the current drought. Around it is a wetlands area, an animal refuge.

Between the lakes and me, between my hills and the distant hills of Hemet and Perris, is the 60 freeway. It is ever growing and ever too small for the volume of cars it supports. When we moved here ten years ago, we would see only a few cars on the road. We drove to Joshua Tree often because it was a pleasant drive. But 909 is in-between. It's in-between where people live and where they want to be, apparently. Now on Sunday afternoons, the freeway is jammed with automobiles, platinum blondes in BMWs, SUVs pulling jet skis, Jeeps with three-inch lift kits, sporty purple cars with spoilers and decals of Calvin peeing on someone or thing. The traffic backs up like a bad septic system and does not move. I don't leave the ranch during these hours. I have come to believe that the highway must be their destination. All of those people have left home to be *there*, on the 60, in 909.

I can see them now, in their air-conditioned boxes, from where I sit on Monk. They are little specks and that's how I like it. For them 909 is the 60 or the 10. For me it's these rugged hills. Hills that defy human occupation. Hills that are not on the way to anywhere. Hills that will let you know if you're welcome. 909.

Percival Everett is the author of seventeen books of fiction. Among them are the novels *American Desert*, *Erasure*, *Glyph*, *Watershed* and *God's Country*. He has received awards from the American Academy of Arts and Letters, the Hurston/Wright Foundation and the Fellowship of Southern Writers

Everett is professor of English at the University of Southern California. He lives with his wife on a small ranch outside Los Angeles and on Vancouver Island, British Columbia.

the line

by Rubén Martínez

Years ago, I wrote several dispatches from the border at Tijuana, easily the most famous crossing along the two-thousand-mile long line. On many occasions, I hung out at the famous *cancha*, a soccer field that runs alongside the border just a mile from downtown. All there was back then was a scraggly fence, perforated in too many places to count. On a bluff a hundred yards north border patrol jeeps were perched day and night.

Through the dusty heat of day, *la cancha* was empty. But as soon as the sun set, it turned into a veritable migrant fiesta. A great crowd gathered at the fence and began organizing the evening's expeditions. The migrants came from all over Mexico and Central America, and as far away as China, Iran, Pakistan. Packs of lone men, unshaven, dusty-haired, carrying only the clothes on their backs or small, cheap vinyl bags filled with just a handful of belongings. And families, entire families, from grandmothers with crinkled faces and braided white hair down to wide-eyed tots in arms.

The crowd gave rise to a mini-economy of vendors exploit-
ing the migrants' last-minute shopping needs. Hawkers pushed
everything from booze and running shoes to girlie magazines and
sheets of plastic for that unforeseen thunderstorm. Grandmothers
stood over coal-fired stoves stirring great steaming pots of pozole or
sizzling *carne asada*, hominy stew and grilled beef. Prostitutes offered
farewell trysts.

Music blared from boom boxes borrowing juice that ran
through a few dozen extension cords hooked up to a socket in someone's living room a couple of hundred yards away, or directly from
the fraying, sparking wires hanging above our heads. And there were
the great migrant soccer matches, featuring intense battles between
rival regions, states and hometowns throughout the republic, which
gave la cancha its name. Zacatecas vs. San Luis Potosí, Michoacán vs.
Saltillo, Durango vs. Tamaulipas.

Goooooooaaaaalllll!

It was a fiesta back then, like a Fourth of July barbecue or a
Sixteenth of September fiesta; everyone was celebrating in anticipation of crossing. Back then, chances were better than fifty-fifty that
you would get across on your first attempt. And even if you were
nabbed by the *migra*, you'd surely get across on your second try,
probably that same night.

Later, after people had eaten, scored a few goals or a blowjob
in the nearby bushes, the coyotes would gather crews of twenty-five
or more migrants, sometimes many more. The coyotes would huddle
among themselves, drawing straws to see which route each team
would take. There were hundreds of ancient footpaths in the hills
above Tijuana, deep ruts carved over the decades by a million migrant
footsteps.

All at once, the crews would move out, hundreds of men,

women and children streaming across the chaparral-dotted hills. The Border Patrol would spring into action, but the gringos would quickly be overwhelmed by the massive tide.

Goooooaaaaallllll!

Sure, it was dangerous sometimes, especially along the line in Texas, where migrants had to ford the trickster-currents of the muddy Bravo. But back then migrants were more likely to get robbed or beaten by border bandits than die of exposure in the middle of the desert.

The border wasn't a border. The line was broken. It was an idea, not a thing.

And then the idea became a reality. In the early '90s, California was in a deep recession. A lot of union jobs had been lost. The Firestone and Goodyear tire plants shut down, as did the last of the old iron and steel works, and aerospace companies laid off tens of thousands of workers. People were angry, and then-governor Pete Wilson looked back in time for inspiration. To the Great Depression and the "repatriation" of hundreds of thousands of Mexican workers. To the postwar recession and Operation Wetback, which deported hundreds of thousands more. And then *la crisis* sent a fresh flood of refugees north. Suddenly Wilson, a Republican who'd always sold himself as friendly to Mexico and Mexicans, a man who, in fact, once had an undocumented woman clean his house, pointed his finger southward.

"They keep coming!" He declared.

He hated the migrants now. Narco-satanic hordes were at the gates. He swore that he would draw a line in the sand that no Wetback would ever cross.

American politicos have paid lip-service to "holding the line" at the southern border for the better part of the twentieth century, beginning in the days of the massive migration spawned by the Mexican Revolution of 1910-17. But in 1994, the rhetoric took the form of concrete, steel, arc lamps, infrared cameras and goggles, seismic and laser sensors and even U.S. soldiers with M-16s offering "tactical support" to a greatly expanded Border Patrol. Operation Gatekeeper sought to block the decades-old illegal crossing at San Diego-Tijuana with a twelve-foot-high steel wall that runs inland twelve miles from the coast. At night, it is lit a harsh amber. The glow that falls from the gigantic light towers straddles the line for several hundred yards in each direction, meaning that the gringo light actually falls on Mexican territory-illegal light as it were, but the Mexican government has never complained about it, or, the constant noise pollution from the helicopters on patrol.

The migrants have complained, though. How they hated the governor of California. "Pito" Wilson, they called him, "*pito*" for "whistle," but also, in Mexico, for "penis." During the 1994 World Cup, Wilson was on hand to inaugurate a match at the Rose Bowl in Los Angeles. Among the hundred thousand people in the stands, there were at least sixty thousand Mexicans, Salvadorans, Guatemalans, Nicaraguans, Hondurans, Columbians, Chileans, Uruguayans, Brazilians, migrants each and every one. Wilson stepped up to the microphone. But no one heard a single word he said over the boos, whistles, and chorus shouting "Pito! Pito!" in great rhythmic waves.

Goooaaaallll!

Pete Wilson has gone, but one thing remains from his nativist legacy.

After years of lobbying Washington to help the Golden State beat back the illegals, the federal government obliged with the new fence at Tijuana. To cross into California today, you have to go

east of the fence. You have to hike in total darkness, through mountains that block out the beacon of city-light from San Diego. You take
a long walk in the dark.

Rubén Martínez was born in Los Angeles and is an Emmy Award-winning
journalist, poet and performer. He was a Loeb Fellow at Harvard University
and an editor for the Pacific News Service. In 2002, he received a literary fellowship from the Lannan Foundation.

Martínez is the author of *Crossing Over: A Mexican Family on the Migrant Trail*
and *The Other Side: Notes from the New L.A., Mexico City and Beyond*. His
newest book is *The New Americans* (The New Press, 2004), a companion to
the PBS television series detailing the lives of migrant families.

Flirting with urbanismo

by Patt Morrison

To all of you who say—with an annoying tone of pride, I must add—"Oh, I've never seen downtown Los Angeles," I say, "Oh yes, you have."

You've seen City Hall, but you thought it was the Daily Planet building in *Superman*, or the Capitol in *The West Wing*, or, my favorite, the Vatican in *The Thorn Birds*.

You've seen the streets of downtown in *Cagney and Lacey* and *Phone Booth* and *Ghostbusters* and just about every cop show and movie with a few seconds of urban grime, but you thought they were in Manhattan 1980 or Chicago 1930. The first feature-length film ever made in Los Angeles was about an oversexed Turkish pasha, and it was filmed in back of a Chinese laundry in downtown.

Some of the most deliciously nasty hate mail I've ever gotten was when I took pleasure in pointing out that the *echt* "New York" apartment house exterior in *Seinfeld* is, as a matter of fact, a building a few miles west of downtown L.A. New Yorkers acted like I'd told them the Statue of Liberty was a foreigner. (Psst, she is—and French, too.)

Personally, I think all those painted curbs that read "taxi zone" in a downtown where free-range taxis are scarcer than snowstorms are there simply to give the locals the pleasure of seeing New Yorkers stand there with their arms foolishly upraised.

There are lots of reasons to be fond of downtown Los Angeles, not the least of which is—it's us.

Downtown is the perfect plastic heart of a plastic city—plastic in the meaning of changeable, moldable. Its blocks are the most versatile, and thus the most filmed in the world; it can play almost anything—just as Angelenos can make themselves into what they wish to be.

So I ask you, why do people disdain downtown? Or why, like Santa Claus, won't they even believe it exists?

Maybe because it's urban the way a studio backlot is urban; every street you cross is utterly different from the streets on either side of it. At Main Street it's Skid Row squalor. At Spring Street— originally Primavera, "Spring" in Spanish, bestowed by the surveyor Edward Ord to try to get in good with a Mexican girl he was courting, a girl he called his "Springtime"—at Spring, it's gold-leaf officialdom: CalTrans, the state courts. Cross Broadway and you're into the raucous Latin American mercantile fest of twenty-four-hour wedding chapels, the entire line of Virgin of Guadalupe goods, expensive quinceañera dresses and cheap almost-gold jewelry. By Hill Street you can frequent the Civic Center subway stop (the cleanest place in Los Angeles), the dazzle of the jewelry district, or the splendor of the Biltmore Hotel, the place the Beatles had to be helicoptered into for some shut-eye during their first American tour.

I once attended a dinner for John Updike at the California Club. The club was founded more than a century ago by the city's elite, and while it *is* downtown, valet parking back in the sheltered porte-cochere means no one must actually set foot on the street to go inside, and I sometimes wonder whether the vast doors fronting Flower Street were installed merely to meet the fire code; I've never seen anyone walk through them.

Anyway, as the evening wore on, Updike asked about returning to his hotel—the Biltmore, whose back door is about a block or so from the California Club's back door. Is it safe, he wondered aloud, to walk?

He must have been talking to some of those west-side weenies, huddling fearfully out there in the 310 area code—people who go to Paris more often than they go to downtown L.A.

It's an urban legend with perhaps some nucleus of truth that in the uneasy days that followed the 1992 riots, the west-of-Sepulveda do-gooders steeled themselves and did come downtown to volunteer to help, but it is an unshakable urban legend that they did it in rented cars, so that no harm might come to their seven-series Beemers.

D owntown is now back in vogue, I hear. The Diz—the Walt Disney Concert Hall—is irresistible. The new cathedral is up and running, looking like a house of God on the inside and a house of correction on the outside. As for the Central Library, restored after the 1986 arson fires, Philip Johnson, the architect, thinks it is simply the greatest building in downtown: "In fact, whenever I think of Los Angeles, I see that library." It's a place to take people who think L.A.'s only culture is in a Petri dish, for the pleasure of hearing their jaws hit their sternums.

Everyone wants to restore downtown.

Restore it to what?

Downtown L.A. has had a fleeting incarnation but a durable resonance, the way the Wild West frontier America existed only a few decades in real life, but has lasted a hundred years and more in the nation's imagination, its film and fiction.

Los Angeles is a city built by centrifugal forces, and what's in the center of a centrifuge? Not much. The L.A. centrifuge flung us, year after year, farther and farther from the core of the city.

L.A.'s essential character has always been suburban, as far back as the land-grant days. What else is a rancho but a suburb, an independent, self-sustaining little town, possessed of granary and tannery, smithy and buttery? A man could ride from rancho to rancho as he might ride from village to village elsewhere in the world.

Downtowns are made by demography more than by geography. Americans have always been a little leery of cities. Thomas Jefferson, an otherwise rational man, wrote of them as "painful objects of vice and wretchedness," whereas in the countryside, "our societies, if not refined, are rational, moral, and affectionate at least."

The demographics of other cities were poor, foreign, working class, immigrant. New York's tenements, Chicago's, crammed with Jewish and Irish and Polish newcomers, clinging to those of like culture and language.

But the immigrants who came to Los Angeles for well over a half-century were middle-class men and women. They had money and skills and education and some very clear ideas of what they wanted: a Southern California R-1 paradise.

Live downtown? In an apartment? You think I traveled all this way by wagon/ship/train to reach this glorious sunshine to cram myself into some dark, little flat? Sure, downtown's a nice place to work, but who'd want to live there?

The Great God of Real Estate encouraged this diaspora. In the 1920s, six thousand electric cars left downtown every day for the four suburban counties, making the notion of living *here* and working *there* no more arduous than telecommuting is now.

Angelenos did work and shop downtown, assiduously. Edward Weston worked in a downtown photo studio, touching up negatives—a step up from his previous job, going door to door taking pictures of kids, pets and even dead relatives. Charles Bukowski sorted mail at the downtown post office and made up dirty words to match ZIP codes to keep from being bored to death.

Even into the 1960s, shopping in the great mercantile *maisons* of Robinson's and Bullock's on Seventh Street was an occasion and a great treat.

We suburban strangers obeyed the rules of the scary city. Even now, you can tell an Angeleno from a resident of any other great city: We're the ones standing meekly on a downtown curb in the dead, dark midnight, waiting for the "walk" sign to turn green. We know that jaywalking is a serious California crime, as Ronald Reagan's attorney general, Ed Meese, found out. Just before Reagan was sworn in as president, the LAPD gave Meese a ten-dollar ticket for jaywalking. Meese ignored it—and five years later, L.A. law reached all the way to the U.S. Justice Department to find Meese and make him pay.

Oh, we had a little flirtation with urbanismo, and we're having one again. The Loft People have moved into downtown; they walk their dogs and sip coffee pavement-side. Restaurants serve dinner until at least the 10 o'clock news; the skyline no longer goes dark at 6 P.M. The penthouse of the Metropolitan Water District headquarters was where the city's chief water engineer, William Mulholland, lived for years, and where, as another second-hand civic truth has it, actor

Nicolas Cage lived for a while. (When the time comes for kids and such, I expect, the loft folks will find their way out to the 626 and the 818 regions, the 310, maybe even the 714.)

We probably manage to get along here in L.A. because there's always been room to keep moving. House too small? Buy a new one. Don't like your neighbor? Don't even care to know your neighbor? There's always somewhere else to go.

Why do you suppose there are so few parks in L.A.? The ruthless gold standard of real estate is one reason: Why put to public use something you can sell? Another reason: This is a city where everyone means to have his own personal, private park—right outside his back door.

It's why we've segregated shopping districts far from nice neighborhoods almost as strictly as we segregated apartment-ridden neighborhoods—they bring urbanity just too close.

I shared the stage a while ago with Pete Hamill, the New York columnist and author, talking about L.A. versus New York—and in a very civil fashion, too, I must say. Hamill was going on and on about the charms of being able to walk out your front door and hoof it to the newsstand or the grocery store.

"Pete," I said, "In Los Angeles, if you live close enough to walk to the grocery store, it's time to move."

⁓

The swift abandonment of downtown for the suburbs was actually what saved the place.

Anywhere else, downtown real estate would be so valuable that whole streets would be built up and torn down a dozen times in a century. Not here. Downtown L.A. reminds me of Pompeii, except the people got out before the eruption. Downtown has block after block of the most exquisite, unspoiled Beaux Arts buildings in the country, all beloved of filmmakers, some as old as Queen Victoria's corset, some built when FDR put Al Capone out of the booze business.

Commercial property values downtown are more capricious than the Newport-Inglewood Fault, as downtown landlords from Japanese investors to the Duke of Westminster have learned. But if there ever was a house in Los Angeles that went for less money than it was bought for, no homeowner would admit to it—he'd have to leave the state.

All that having been said, downtown is part circus, part museum—everywhere, something worth looking at:

- The Bradbury building, an undisputed urban treasure and an official national landmark, was designed at the urging of a Ouija board after the man tapped to build it consulted his eight-year-old dead brother, Mark, and was told, Take the job.
- The hotels where genius once stopped over: the down-and-out Alexandria, where Sarah Bernhardt and Enrico Caruso bedded— separately—and where Mary Pickford, Charlie Chaplin, D.W. Griffith and Doug Fairbanks put their heads together and created United Artists; and the Biltmore, where Cedric Gibbons designed the Oscar statuette on a hotel napkin.
- The Oviatt building, the biggest commercial project that glass artist Rene Lalique ever undertook, was a very *flossy* 1920s men's store, founded by James Oviatt, a fugitive from life in Utah. He lived above the shop in a penthouse to which he imported sand from the South of France to create his own beach. There's a wonderful restaurant there now, and still some of the Lalique chic, which is why the flying-escargot scene from *Pretty Woman* was filmed there.

- L.A., with more hills than Rome, was a city of funiculars, and the last survivor of these is Angels Flight, with its persimmon-colored wooden cars rattling up Bunker Hill—if the city's timid underwriters ever let it reopen.
- The Los Angeles Conservancy's "Last Remaining Seats" tour of the pastry-tube curlicue-and-gilt-adorned downtown theatres, some of them predating the exotic movie houses of Hollywood Boulevard.
- The last surviving cafeteria of the Clifton's chain, built by a man who asked patrons to pay what they thought the food was worth. He also nearly got murdered investigating official corruption—truly one of God's good citizens, and innocents.
- The palimpsest city. On the sides of old brick buildings you can still make out painted ads, such as the old Army and Navy Store's as you drive north on Main Street, and ads for hotels that once offered steam heat and services for ten bucks a week.

⌒⫘⌒

There's so much more that enchants me—the tiled caverns of Union Station, where I can now confess I used to roller skate (on plastic wheels, okay?) . . . the early-morning enticements of the garment district and the flower market . . . the hilariously idiotic Triforium, a civic culture venture that failed, a three-story, three-legged jukebox north of City Hall that's never worked properly, probably because the designer sold the city the "sculpture" but kept the instructions.

And there's a certain acute-angled corner of a building in the Wells Fargo Plaza where I can stand and tilt my head back and—like a little kid wanting the Ferris wheel to go faster—almost enjoy feeling like I'm about to lose my lunch, gazing at the infinite height of it.

Keep in mind, if you're getting neck strain, that L.A. was the first city created in the age of wheeled transportation—the streetcar, the Model-T. Why do you think businesses hoisted their signs up so high, so big, so unreadable from the sidewalk? Because you're not supposed to be walking.

Just kidding. I hear walking is coming back, too.

Only please, wherever you stroll—don't jaywalk.

Patt Morrison is a writer and columnist for the *Los Angeles Times*; she is a member of two *Times* reporting teams that won Pulitzer Prizes for coverage of the 1992 riots and the city's 1994 earthquake. Her 2001 book, *Río L.A., Tales from the Los Angeles River*, spent six weeks on the bestseller list, and was ranked as one of the year's best in the *Los Angeles Times Book Review*.

Morrison is a regular commentator on National Public Radio and has won six Emmys and four Golden Mike awards as founding host and commentator on *Life & Times Tonight*, the current affairs program on KCET. She lives in Los Angeles.

www.pattmorrison.com.

waters of tranquility

by Carolyn See

I t's miniature, it's a play toy, it's childlike, it's deceiving, it's very
beautiful. The Lake Shrine of the Self-Realization Fellowship
hides behind hedges on Sunset Boulevard about half a mile up
from the beach. It's been there for fifty years, since an immensely
engaging yogi named Paramahansa Yogananda got the idea and put
the place together as a shrine to world peace.

There's a lake with a flock of mud hens and swans and some
overweight and self-indulgent Chinese carp. A rowboat and, moored
to the shore, a two-story houseboat painted spanking white. Around
the lake, a gravel path, and up on every side of the path, the most
eccentric gardens possible.

The only thing there is to do is walk around that lake . . .
and around it again . . . and around it again. Eating or sunbathing or
raucous frolicking aren't allowed, although weddings are all right.
You see them taking place every once in a while on the patch of lawn
in front of the Gandhi World Peace Memorial, or hear snatches of

ceremonies floating out in the air from an old-fashioned windmill that looks a lot like an old Van de Kamp's bakery. Less is more; less gets the point across. A little sign that pokes up from a flower bed, looking very much like it should say BURMA SHAVE, says, instead, EVERYTHING ELSE CAN WAIT, BUT OUR SEARCH FOR GOD CANNOT WAIT. And over by the Rose Garden at the entrance there are monuments to the five great human religions: Islam, Christianity, Judaism, Buddhism, Hinduism. But these monuments are peach-colored cement, or sandstone, just about tall enough to sit on, with little metal plaques stuck on. You don't have to look up to these things; they're like stone children, maybe four feet tall. What if, in all our striving, we and our beliefs were still childish, childlike, largely unformed, just little somethings poking up into the universe?

The people who come here don't ponder this stuff. I used to come here with boyfriends for romantic afternoons. Benches dot the path around the lake and everywhere here you see lovers entwined in long, slow, almost motionless embraces. Determined meditators keep their eyes closed, backs straight, always a little silly-looking, I'm sorry to say. Unemployed dads shepherd their kids around the lake and around again. Tourists from Germany, France, Russia, Japan and India clump around in raggedy groups taking pictures of each other.

Farther up on this hill, the modern Fellowship has constructed a great big new temple in sparkling white and brightest gold. On Sundays, the place is always packed, but Paramahansa Yogananda himself was the one who thought up the Lake Shrine—the houseboat, the windmill, the baby waterfall with a statue of Krishna standing just above it, the bigger waterfall with Christ peering over, the tiny statue of St. Francis, the swans, the shining carp, the turtle army, the terraces and beds so dizzily cramped with flowers both rare and common that in the spring you could faint from the scent alone. What a guy, that Yogananda!

My life partner, John Espey, and I had lived in Topanga Canyon for years before we moved to Pacific Palisades. I guess we'd learned to think of nature as harsh and flammable, heavy on the rattlesnakes. It was interesting to go from clearing brush to that peaceable and temperate walk around the lake. Wasn't it just too pretty for words? Kind of a sissy place? Beautiful, of course, but not real, not like . . . life?

John was very sick for two years. He'd walk around the lake, slowly, turning up his nose at the signs, because he was an atheist. But loving the rest of it.

He wanted to die at home, and that process is harder than it sounds. His family differed drastically on how best to take care of him, and my daily response to that was rage.

Every day, I'd swing on over to the Lake Shrine, right on the brink of murdering one well-meaning relative or another, and make the first circle, swearing, muttering oaths and imprecations, sneering at whoever got in my way. By the second time around, I'd remembered why I was there, how I was losing the man I loved most in the world. I'd lean against trees and weep, sit on those benches and sob. The third time around, I'd hear myself asking for *courage, steadfastness, compassion!* The fourth time around, I could walk, and watch.

In the scheme of things where a major religion only rates a four-foot monument, a single human death may be no more than a fall of one flower, one tweaked leaf. There are so many more! And life itself may be no more than a play toy, a few Burma-Shave signs in the universe. But blazing, amazing, for all that. You can see that at the Lake Shrine. I know I did.

Carolyn See is the author of five novels, including *The Handyman* and *Golden Days*. Her most recent book is *Making a Literary Life*. She is the Friday morning book reviewer for *The Washington Post* and is on the board of PEN Center USA West. She has a Ph.D. in American literature from UCLA.

See's awards include the prestigious *Los Angeles Times* Robert Kirsch Award (1993) for her body of work and a Guggenheim Fellowship in fiction. She lives in Pacific Palisades.

www.carolynsee.com.

an ordinary place

by D.J. Waldie

Where I live is where most Californians live—in a tract house on a block of more tract houses in a neighborhood hardly distinguishable from the next and all of them extending as far as the street grid allows. My exact place on the grid is at the extreme southeast corner of Los Angeles County, but that's mostly by accident. While I reside in Lakewood, I live in suburbia, where my home might almost be anywhere.

I've lived here my whole life, in the 957-square-foot house my parents bought in 1946 when the idea of suburbia was brand new, and no one knew what would happen when thirty-five thousand working-class husbands and wives—young and so inexperienced— were thrown together without any instruction manual and expected to make a fit place to live. What happened after was the usual redemptive mix of joy and tragedy.

At least their suburbia wasn't an oil company camp in Oklahoma, a walk-up tenement in a crabbed Midwestern town, or a shack at the end of a dirt road somewhere in the border South. There are Californians who don't regard tract houses as places of pilgrimage, but my parents and their friends in Lakewood did. They weren't ironists. They were grateful for the comforts of their not-quite-middle-class life. For those who came to Lakewood, the aspiration wasn't for more but only for enough.

It's slightly more than fifty years since an idling road grader waited while the last harvesters worked in the fields before it dug into the empty ground. That was the start of a long line of machines that scraped the truck farms, chicken ranches, and orange groves of Los Angeles County into suburbia. Despite everything that was ignored or squandered in its making, I believe a kind of dignity was gained. More men than just my father have said to me that living in the suburbs gave them a life made whole and habits that did not make them feel ashamed. They knew what they found and lost.

Mostly, they found enough space to reinvent themselves, although some of them found that reinvention went badly, that in making their place they had left parts of their life unfinished. Some of them, the men particularly, gave up what little adolescence they retained after the Depression and the second world war. That loss made them seem remote to their sons and daughters.

In 1960 in Lakewood, almost forty percent of the population was under fourteen. An ordinary block of forty-two houses might have a hundred children, and in the summer, they would spend the daylight and early evening hours outdoors in loose, happy packs.

Urban planners tell me that my neighborhood was supposed to have been bulldozed away years ago to make room for a better paradise of the ordinary, and yet these little houses on little lots stubbornly resist, loyal to an idea of how a working-class neighborhood should be made. It's an incomplete idea, but it's still enough to bring out four hundred park sports coaches in the fall and six hundred to clean up the weedy yards of the frail and disabled on Volunteer Day in April and more than two thousand to sprawl on lawn chairs and blankets to listen to the summer concerts at José del Valle Park. I don't live in a tear-down neighborhood, but one that makes some effort to build itself up.

Suburbia isn't all of a piece, of course, and there are plenty of toxic places to live in gated enclaves and the McMansion wastelands of Los Angeles. Places like that have too much—isolation in one and mere square footage in the other—but, paradoxically, not enough. Specifically, they don't have enough of the play between life in public and life in private that I see choreographed by the design of Lakewood. There's an education in narrow streets when they are bordered by sidewalks and a shallow setback of twenty feet of lawn in front of unassuming houses set close enough together that their density is about seven units per acre.

With neighbors just fifteen feet apart, we're easily in each other's lives in Lakewood—across fences, in front yards and even through the thin, stucco-over-chicken-wire of house walls. You don't have to love all of the possibilities for civility handed to us roughly by the close circumstances of working-class suburbia, but you have to love enough of them, or you live, as some do, numbly or in a state of permanent, mild fury.

I once thought my suburban education was an extended lesson in how to get along with other people. Now, I think the lesson isn't neighborliness; it's humility. Growing up in Lakewood, the only sign of a man's success I can remember was the frequency with which a new car appeared in a neighbor's driveway. Even today, it's hard to claim status in Lakewood through personal gain (in our peculiar American way) because this is a suburb where life is still pretty much the same for everybody, no matter how much you think you're worth.

Lakewood's modesty keeps me here. When I stand at the head of my block and look north, I see a pattern of sidewalk, driveway and lawn, set between parallel low walls of house fronts that aspires to be no more than harmless. We are living in a time of great harm now, and I wish that I had acquired all the graces my neighborhood gives.

My neighborhood was the place where suburban stories were first mass-produced for the hopeful millions of mid-twentieth century Los Angeles. Then, they were stories for displaced Okies and Arkies, Jews who knew the pain of exclusion, Catholics who thought they did, and anyone white with a steady job. Left out, of course, were many thousands of others.

Today, suburban stories still begin here, except the anxious, hopeful people who tell them are as mixed in their colors and ethnicities as our whole, mongrel California. The Public Policy Institute of California reported recently that Lakewood had one of the highest rates of ethnic diversification among California cities. I continue to live here with anticipation because I want to find out what happens next to these new narrators of suburban stories.

Loyalty is the last habit that anyone would impute to those of us who live in suburbia; we're supposed to be so dissatisfied. But I'm not unusual in living in Lakewood for all the years I have. Nearly twenty-seven percent of the city's residents have lived here thirty years or more. Perhaps, like me, they've found a place that permits restless people to be still. The primal mythmakers of Los Angeles are its real estate agents, and one of them told me that Lakewood attracted aspirant homebuyers because "it's in the heart of the metroplex." Or, maybe, it's just in the heart. I live here because Lakewood is adequate to the demands of my desire, although I know there's a price to pay.

A Puritan strain in American culture is repelled by desires like mine, and has been since a brilliant young photographer named William A. Garnett, working for the Lakewood Park corporation, took a series of aerial photographs in 1950 that look down on the vulnerable wood frames of the houses the company was putting up at the rate of five hundred a week. Even after fifty years, those beautiful and terrible photographs are used to indict suburbia. Except you can't see the intersection of character and place from an altitude of five hundred feet, and Garnett never came back to experience everyday life on the ground.

The everyday isn't perfect. It confines some and leads some astray into contempt or nostalgia, but it saves others. I live where I live in California because the weight of my everyday life here is a burden I want to carry.

D.J. Waldie is the author of *Holy Land: A Suburban Memoir*; *Real City: Downtown Los Angeles Inside/Out*; and *Where We Are Now: Notes from Los Angeles*. His book reviews and commentary appear in the *Los Angeles Times*. He is a contributing writer for *Los Angeles* magazine.

Waldie lives in Lakewood in the house his parents bought in 1946.

almost home

by Gerald Haslam

Near the southern end of California's Great Central Valley, we veer east from Interstate 5, then travel a two-lane past the green spokes of agricultural fields, oil pumps salaaming in the middle of some. We pass a shaggy, uncultivated plot—ragamuffin amidst Lord Fauntleroys. But it isn't a remnant of indigenous rangeland because, like the farms, it is covered with non-native plants; everything here, it seems—weeds and crops and people—comes from elsewhere.

Wind that smells vaguely of chemicals tugs at our car. "Look," says my wife, pointing at a lone kite pumping its wings above another unplanted tract. Beyond, a dust devil swerves and pirouettes, faint as a ghost, and our car rushes toward a mirage flooding the pavement: like most of California we pursue the illusion of water.

Few of the fields here boast houses, for this is the terrain of corporate agriculture, with the richest farmers working in far-off boardrooms while brown men and women irrigate, plow and harvest. Some family farmers remain, of course, and they live on the land and work with the laborers, who in turn reside in farm labor camps or ranch cabins or tiny towns on the margin, *debajo del puente* . . . reminders of our shared past.

Well ahead of us, treeless, tan hills begin to emerge from haze, hills steaming constantly as though Hell has sprung a leak; hot vapors are pumped underground there to melt thick petroleum so it can be harvested. At the foot of those hills hides a town—a few dark hints of trees betrays its location—but we know it well: Oildale, a community now contiguous with north Bakersfield. Then we discern a distant building, then two, then the silvery towers of an oil refinery.

I turn to Jan and smile. "Almost home," I say.

She smiles back: "Almost home."

My great-great grandparents—he a *vaquero*, she a seamstress—first entered the Valley in the 1850s when they migrated north from Mexico. I was born here in 1937, married here in 1961, and my wife and I will one day be buried here with kin and dear friends . . . like our neighbors—from Oklahoma, Texas, Missouri and Arkansas, mostly—who became extended family.

Some of them were oral virtuosos: One older man said of my boyhood chum Merle Haggard, "That kid's wild as a acre a snakes." Another neighbor described an unbeatable high school sprinter as "Faster'n green grass through a white goose." When I went to work as a summer replacement in the oilfields, the boss winked at my dad as he said, "That clumsy kid of yours could fall out of a hole. That's some kind of boy you got there, Speck."

In some ways the setting, not the people, dominates. Oildale is part of one of the most productive unnatural landscapes in the history of the world: transported water, chemical agriculture, steam-infused petroleum and more than a little political chicanery produce jobs for many, wealth for few. Despite the absence of buildings, the nearby fields and hills are as developed as downtown Bakersfield.

As a kid, I used to think everywhere else smelled funny—no sulfuric belch of crude oil in most other places, no texture to their air. From my earliest memory, everything hereabouts seemed dry but not desolate. Less than six inches of rain fall most years, yet the area still teems with life: ants, lizards, rabbits, coyotes, hawks—the whole chain. Long ago there were pronghorns and elk and grizzlies, too. And many Yokuts, native people.

When Thomas Baker migrated here in 1863, long before he made his field available to travelers, it was called Kern Island. The island—*islands*, really—were formed by the entrapped distributary channels of the Kern River, whose water did not flow out of the Great Valley to San Francisco Bay, but instead puddled nearby in two lakes—8,300-acre Kern and 4,000-acre Buena Vista—plus a complex of wetlands, marshes amidst desert. Only Buena Vista Lake survived into my childhood, then it, too, was gone.

During those years, I often rode my bike a mile from our neighborhood to an unreal realm I called "Tarzan's House"—great shading trees, dangling vines, dense brush through which animals scurried. And icy water. The Kern River and its riparian forest were our fishing hole, our swimming pool, our jungle . . . and as startling in that barren setting as an unexpected flashbulb.

In 1950, I stood on a levee and watched brown water surge bridge-high out of the Sierra. My future wife, whose family lived near the levee in a section called Riverview, viewed the river in her house.

Neither of us could know we were witnessing the last of the floods that over millennia had deposited the alluvial soil upon which the agriculture empire has been built.

Four years later, Isabella Dam was completed upstream—ostensibly for flood control, actually to provide more water for agribusiness—and the riparian forest began to die. By the time I returned home from the army in 1960, that woodland's remains stood like unwrapped mummies, and the channel had become a long sand trap. My children and I walked there a few times, but they couldn't imagine the setting I described, so I tucked it back into memory.

Local folks have recently lobbied for the return of year-round flows, and some water has been granted them, so there is reason to hope that future generations might one day know something of the wondrous natural world that once hosted the Yokuts . . . and my pals, and me. In my heart—in that interior world where most of us really live—I still visit Tarzan's House, and the vacant lot where horned toads scurried, and the treeless bluffs where adolescent necking thrived.

Although all our family there is now gone, my wife and I return to Oildale frequently because we must, and each time we walk its streets and alleys and fields, we savor them . . . memory and sense merging: "That park, it was an oil sump, remember? I saw a lizard run onto it, then sink. I wanted to cry."

"Didn't that kid Cootie live there? He was killed in Vietnam."

"Look, that's Bud and Katie's dad sitting on the porch. Man, how old is he now?"

On those visits, too, we especially love to sit on a pal's porch, watch doves drinking in the gutter and view orange-and-blue sunsets spectacular as the northern lights. We know that air pollution creates those colors, but in Oildale everything is bittersweet. It is also almost as I remember it, almost home.

Gerald Haslam is the author or editor of twenty-seven books, most of which are set in his native Great Central Valley. His *Coming of Age in California* was named one of the West's one hundred most important nonfiction twentieth-century books by a *San Francisco Chronicle* readers' poll. His most recent novel, *Straight White Male*, won the Western States Book Award in 2000.

Haslam lives in Penngrove.

www.geraldhaslam.com.

my little saigon

by Anh Do

D o you live in Little Saigon?"
        I can tell you exactly how many times I've been asked that: 112.

People—strangers, tourists, disc jockeys—they all wonder about this place smack in the middle of Westminster, a bedroom community in Orange County. Where the heck is it, folks want to know. Is the population large? Are the signs in English?

Even my family, those from the old country, pose questions.

It comes up—No. 113—when I call back to Vietnam and chat with my cousin, a baker at a big hotel. He asks for my address. Then he says: "Is there anything similar between Saigon and Little Saigon?"

Sure. Let me tell you.

This turf of mine emerged in the late 1970s, when a refugee opened up the first business, a pharmacy stocking Band-

Aids and Tiger Balm, along Bolsa Avenue. Then came the first strip mall, and under that brown-shingle roof, my father, on impulse, signed on to lease a room. He had started the first Vietnamese-language newspaper in the United States, inking accent marks by hand and distributing the initial two thousand copies door-to-door.

Others needed space, too.

Around us, florists, markets, travel agencies and hair salons soon dotted what was once strawberry fields. Clinics sprung up after refugee doctors went back to school to earn U.S. degrees. Then came the first of Little Saigon's eighty-something beef noodle restaurants, promising fulfillment for $4.50 a bowl.

Tens of thousands of immigrants had crossed the ocean at the end of the Vietnam War and church sponsors resettled them in places like Arkansas and Pennsylvania. But those states were too isolated, too cold. The refugees began streaming to Southern California, seduced by the sun and block after block of buildable land.

Our family paper wrote about them, about how they struggled to take driving tests and to understand strange vocabulary words at parent-teacher conferences. And about how these men and women, missing their old haunts, transformed tiny homes on the edge of town into ornate Buddhist temples.

We could not afford a house in 1978. The six of us—my parents and four children—squeezed into a three-bedroom rental, which grew even tighter as my Dad welcomed one old friend after another, and their wives and kids, too. They were the boat people, fleeing pirates on the high seas as they escaped Vietnam and seeking haven with families that had started over.

We were never alone.

For dinner, we sat down with huge crowds eating huge

meals of catfish, jasmine rice and sweet and sour tomato soup, as all the youngsters grabbed for chopsticks before they ran out. My only brother shared his picture books and his toys with homesick men, who smoked and drank while playing with him.

Yet they soon saw, as we all did, that memories of old would return anew.

A group of civic-minded leaders persuaded local politicos to lobby for a Little Saigon exit off the Garden Grove (22) Freeway. Up went the sign—after some resistance—and in the 1980s, a boom followed.

Around that time, I started Santiago High School, which was one-third Vietnamese, one-third Latino and one-third white. On International Day, we all shared each other's cuisine and we learned each other's dances.

On the weekends, my family would head for a mom-and-pop store, filling our carts with mangos and soybean milk. We'd mingle with shoppers driving in from Riverside and Los Angeles, not finding what they needed in the haze of Chinatown. Outside, ex-soldiers swapped battleground stories, sipping iced coffees at their favorite cafes, trading berets and speaking what they learned from the French who colonized their homeland.

You'd be surprised how many shops we have on this strip, I say over the long-distance line to my cousin.

In fact, Little Saigon, that mile-and-a-half-stretch, has spilled over to neighboring Santa Ana, Garden Grove and Fountain Valley, with more than three thousand Vietnamese-run businesses furiously competing for customers. They offer "buy-one, get-one free" specials for baguettes and mung bean desserts. The area is now a cultural and commercial hub for four hundred thousand Vietnamese scattered across Southern California.

And it's possible to exist here like we existed in Vietnam, without speaking a word of English.

"You have everything you need from the bank to the for-tune teller to Little Saigon Traffic School," I tell my cousin. One difference: Those who don't have drivers' licenses have to memo-rize the bus routes, rather than flag down a bicycle taxi.

Tradition survives. But it's a delicate balance.

I see more and more kids throwing away things written in Vietnamese for comic books and glossy magazines. It's exactly why, today—2004—my family's *Nguoi Viet Daily* newspaper has given birth to *Nguoi Viet 2*, printed in their preferred language: English.

The teenagers with Palm Pilots stand waiting for their moms inside herbal stores, even though they'd much rather be at Nordstrom. Many don't speak Vietnamese. They can't communi-cate with the older workers still trying to master ESL. The booster types push this for better service. We have to "upgrade," the cham-ber reps say, if we're going to attract non-Vietnamese customers.

Some of my countrymen, hearing about this enclave being built, had misgivings. There could be only one Saigon, they say.

"But when I'm inside the market, smelling that familiar smell of fresh fish and fish sauce, I don't think I've ever left Vietnam," my aunt and I tell each other.

You see, her soul lives here. Same with mine.

Anh Do writes an Asian affairs column for the *Orange County Register* and is vice president of business at *Nguoi Viet Daily News*, the oldest and largest Vietnamese-language newspaper in the United States. She is a graduate of the University of Southern California and has studied international relations at Regents College in London and Spanish at the National Autonomous University in Mexico City. Her writing about race, culture and faith has been honored by Columbia University's School of Journalism, the University of Washington's DART award and the Asian American Journalists Association.

Do previously worked at the *Dallas Morning News* and the *Seattle Times* and has reported from India, Mexico, Vietnam, Guatemala, Peru, England and Cuba. She lives in Orange County.

the nicest person in san francisco

by Derek M. Powazek

I was seventeen when I first came to San Francisco. It was 1990 and my dad was attending a conference in Berkeley and I agreed to tag along, under the guise of "checking out UC Berkeley" even though I'd already set my heart on Santa Cruz.

I'd do anything to get up to The Big City, and my dad loved to trap me in a car with him for eight hours so we could have those "father-son bonding" kind of talks.

We took Highway 1 up most of the way. Dad and I in a dark blue BMW 320i (the car I still picture him in, even though he's driven a string of nondescript Hondas since). Just us and the slowly curving road.

I fell asleep immediately and slept soundly from Los Angeles to Los Gatos. I think my dad is still disappointed.

We stopped in San Francisco on our way to Berkeley. Dad asked me where I wanted to go. Where else would a high school kid want to go?

"Haight Ashbury!"

We found a parking meter and were getting out of the car when the specter of drugs first raised its head. My dad hadn't even shut his door and there was this guy in front of him.

"Hey, man. Wanna buy some pot?" said the guy.

"No," said my dad, shutting the door.

"How about some shrooms?"

I giggled. Dad glared at me.

"No."

"Speed?"

"No!"

Dad grabbed me and away we went into the bustle of Haight Street.

I was in awe. All these people. All these colors. It was better than I'd imagined it. I decided then and there that someday I would live here. (Little did I know I'd be living in the Lower Haight five years later, and still call San Francisco my home today.)

When we got back to the car my dad discovered a ticket on his windshield. We'd been in such a panic to escape the walking pharmacy, he'd forgotten to put money in the meter.

Mumbling profanities, my dad led me across Market Street to a burrito joint he knew. There I experienced my first super veggie burrito. I was astounded. I couldn't finish half of it. That burrito shop is a few blocks from my current home.

We grabbed the leftovers and jumped on the bridge to Berkeley, my face plastered to the window, trying to take in every last bit.

The next day my dad was stuck in conferences until 6 P.M. We'd talked about what I'd do when this happened and he was always fuzzy on the details. I think he didn't want me to use his car. That 320i was his baby.

He looked me up and down, took a deep breath, and handed me the keys. As our hands touched and he looked deep within my soul to make sure I was worthy, he said:

"Be good, Derek. And whatever you do, don't go to San Francisco."

In the movie adaptation of my life, those words will boom in full THX sound.

I was supposed to go to UC Berkeley to see the campus. And I actually did. But then it was 1 P.M. and I had time to kill and I sure could go for another one of those burritos. I pulled out the map and I was gone.

The drive from Berkeley to San Francisco over the Bay Bridge is still one of my favorite drives of all time. There's this moment when you pop out of the Treasure Island tunnel and the city just explodes into view. The bridge towers jet up and bang! You can see the whole place all at once: the skyscrapers in the financial district, Coit Tower, all of it.

I cranked the stereo up and the windows down. I was ready for adventure. And I was gonna get it.

Boy was I gonna get it.

I wound my way onto Market Street because it looked like the biggest street on the map. The plan was to go back to Haight Street, and they seemed to connect further down. But then something caught my eye.

"THE PSYCHEDELIC SHOP"

It beckoned to me. It was like a high school idealist magnet.

The outside of the store was painted with swirling colors and covered with cool. I had to go there.

Only, it was on the right side of the street. My heart sank as I passed sign after sign that screamed "No Right Turn." I watched the store fade in my rearview mirror.

But I would not be that easily daunted. Finally I found a place to turn right. I thought I'd just wind my way back.

Now, here would be a good place to mention that I grew up outside of L.A. in an area that, if God had his way, would have been a big, flat desert. When you build a city on a big, flat desert you can afford to make it a big grid, with evenly spaced streets all at nice, comfy, ninety-degree angles. Not so in San Francisco.

There is a grid in that part of town, sure. But Market Street cuts through it at some weird angle that my freedom-addled brain had failed to comprehend.

So I got lost. Real lost. Real fast.

Eventually I got frustrated and thought I'd find the store easier on foot. So I took the first parking space I could find (thirty minutes on the meter—what luck!) and set out for the Psychedelic Shop.

The amazing thing is, I actually found it.

It was worth the hunt. I was lost in rows of tie-dyes, stickers, and pipes. This was the mother of all head shops and I was taking no prisoners. I had a wad of hard-earned summer-job cash in my pocket, and it was going fast.

I picked up a shirt or two and a few stickers and headed for the door. I had a good five minutes to get back to dad's car before the meter expired, and a full two hours to get back to Berkeley. I was gonna be fine.

"Hey, buddy! You like The Dead?"

I looked up. A tall, lanky black man with an itty-bitty pony-tail and an untucked white collared shirt was standing in front of me.

"Yeah, how did you know?"

"Your shirt, man!"

I looked down and remembered I wore my tie-dyed Alice in Wonderland shirt for the big day.

"Oh, yeah."

He made some more small talk, called me "buddy" a lot, and then finally popped the question.

"Say, buddy, you wanna buy some weed?"

My brain raced. I had money. I was in San Francisco. I was on a freedom binge. I looked up and said one of the stupidest things of my entire life.

"Sure!"

The next few moments all happened in a flash. He grabbed me and suddenly we were in a store. I looked up and saw flesh. I scanned back and saw video boxes. A porn store. Great.

He pulled me over into a corner and started pushing a little baggie at me. "Ten dollars," he said, over and over. "Ten dollars."

My head was spinning and my eyes were bugging. I looked over and saw the shopkeeper behind a counter, looking at us. Behind him were black-and-white monitors with security camera feeds on them. All around me was hardcore nudity.

I handed him the ten bucks and turned to escape. He grabbed me hard and started to shove another baggie into my hand. "Five bucks," he said. "Come on. One more. Five bucks."

I guess it was buy one, get one half off day.

I glanced past him to a staircase, leading down from the sec-ond level of the store. I saw a foot. Black shoe. It took a step down.

Blue slacks. Another step. "Take the baggie." Another step. "Five bucks." Another step. Black shoes. Security cameras. Blue slacks. And suddenly one excruciating thought hit me in the face:

Cop.

My God . . . the guy walking down the stairs . . . is a cop.

⚜

My heart pounding in my ears, I turned and ran. I burst out of the store, running blindly down Market Street at top speed. I was sure the cops were after me. I ran until I couldn't any longer, without looking back, into an area I'd later learn is called the Tenderloin.

When I finally stopped and looked around, there were no cops. To this day I'm not sure if the foot I saw in the store belonged to a cop or not. But it didn't matter—I'd escaped.

But in my haste I'd rounded several corners, heading into uncharted territory. It slowly dawned on me. I had no idea where I was. And it was getting late.

I wandered through back streets and avenues looking for that familiar 320i. But every intersection looked the same and, after everything that'd happened, I couldn't remember the name of the street I'd parked on.

At one point I found myself standing at a corner, waiting for the light to change. I looked up and noticed that the two women standing next to me were wearing short black leather skirts and enough makeup to cover Los Angeles. A van pulled up to the corner and one of the women walked over to it. I glanced at the other woman. She glanced at me. I looked down.

A moment later, the woman walked back from the van.

"He wants you instead," she said to her friend.

"Yeah?" said the other one. "Why?"

"Too few teeth," she said, smiling a gap-toothed grin.

The light changed. I ran.

When I finally found my dad's car, the inevitable had happened. There was a parking ticket waiting for me.

As happy as I was to be back in the car, I had a new, frightening vision. My dad and I would return home and he'd get a letter from the San Francisco Department of Parking and Traffic concerning a ticket he received on a day when his car had no business being in San Francisco. I realized I had to pay it now.

I got the address from the ticket, found it on the map, and was off like a shot for the San Francisco County Courthouse.

⌒╫⌒

I got there in minutes. It's amazing how well you can navigate a strange town when you're facing a father's wrath. I parked the car, jumped out, and ran into the building.

Right through a metal detector.

Which I set off.

Damn.

Stunned, I spun around to see a cop with a metal detector wand.

"Please empty your pockets," she said.

I reached into my pocket and felt something unmistakable. Something unthinkable. Something in a little plastic baggie.

I tried not to let my face register the panic. I reached in, very delicately, and removed my wallet, leaving the baggie in my pocket.

I set my wallet on the table and stepped through the metal

detector again. Beep! I set it off again.

"Come on through," she said.

My heart was working overtime. I thought she was gonna search me. But she just ran her magic metal detector wand over me, past my burning pocket, down to my Birkenstocks where they went off again.

"Heh," I stammered. "Metal buckles." I was overjoyed.

She scowled at me and then turned away. "Next!"

I grabbed my wallet, shoved it deep into my pocket, and headed for the ticket counter.

⟲—#—⟳

Upstairs. Downstairs. I finally found my way through the maze of a building to the ticket counter. I waited in line, nervously checking my watch. When I got to the window, I handed the man my ticket. He took one look at me and said, "First time in San Francisco?"

I almost burst into tears. "Yes, sir." I said. "And you wouldn't believe the day I've had."

"Hang in there, kid," he said, taking my twenty-five bucks. "It gets better."

He smiled. I smiled.

"You know," I said, "you're the nicest person I've met in San Francisco."

I walked out of there a new man—a San Franciscan.

And in a flash I was back on the Bay Bridge, through the tunnel, into Berkeley, and into the hotel. I made the drive in thirty minutes. I don't think anyone has ever made it faster, especially in rush-hour traffic.

I ran down the hall and into the room. I collapsed on the bed and let out a sigh. Just then I heard my dad's keys at the door.

"Hi," he said as he came in. "How was Berkeley?"

I rolled over on the bed. "Berkeley? Berkeley was fine, Dad."

Derek M. Powazek is an author and designer from San Francisco. An accomplished performer, he's the leader of the storytelling magazine/movement *Fray* (www.fray.com), which holds true story events all over the world. He also is the author of *San Francisco Stories*, a web site and book of his true tales of life in the city.

Powazek lives in the Cole Valley neighborhood with his fiancée, a nervous dog, an evil cat and a horde of houseplants all named Fred.

www.powazek.com.

the un-california

by Daniel Weintraub

Walk along the pedestrian plaza near the state Capitol some afternoon in the spring or summer, and you're likely to run into an aging man seated at a cheap metal table, eating frozen yogurt from a paper cup. He'll be dressed in rumpled slacks and a loud, short-sleeved shirt and he'll probably be surrounded by friends. If you listen closely, you'll hear him muttering profanities and talking basketball. This will be John Burton, a legend in California politics and the leader of the California Senate, after the governor the most powerful man in state government.

Burton will have no security guard with him, no cops or aides to brush people away. His only defense is his famously foul mouth and what can be, on bad days, a menacing growl. Reporters or citizens alike are equally free to approach him, and chances are, the citizen will get the warmer reception.

Burton's casual bearing is not unusual here, and in fact the people who govern the nation's largest state are surprisingly accessible.

Even Gov. Arnold Schwarzenegger, the megastar and multimillion-aire, has taken to doing lunch on the town, with security unobtrusive enough to allow the occasional visitor to approach for a handshake or a brief chat.

That air of informality is at the heart of Sacramento's charm, although the city's leaders don't seem to recognize it. The mayor and local business honchos are forever pining for "major league status," whatever that means, hoping to be recognized far and wide as some sort of world-class city. They sense, correctly, that to the rest of California, Sacramento is the afterthought capital, the place you stop on the way to someplace else. When I left my native San Diego seventeen years ago to move here to write about state government and politics, friends and family looked at me blankly. Sacramento?

But that's exactly what I like about it. With its two gorgeous rivers—the Sacramento flowing from the north state and the American gurgling down from the Sierra—the city feels more Midwest than California. Huge shade trees line downtown boulevards, creating canopies above the streets of the prewar neighborhoods of brick and stucco homes that surround downtown to the south and east. Its central city, with the exception of a few faded blocks here and there, is vibrant and growing more so, with a mix of business and housing that makes living near where you work more affordable, and more desirable, than in the state's major urban centers.

The climate also is not what most people associate with California, and it has a noticeable effect on the local psyche. The weather is just uneven enough to give residents a sense of the changing seasons and the rhythms they can bring to life, the shared discomfort of dealing with the damp winter cold and the blazing hot summers. Storms that bring snow to the nearby mountains and fill the region's reservoirs are not shunned as unruly intruders but welcomed like old friends. People here realize that water falling from the sky is not an irritant but part of the cycle of life. My children, growing up in Sacramento, have learned that fresh produce doesn't just show up on the grocery shelves but comes from the nearby fields, the result of the risk and hard work of farmers and laborers alike.

The city's distinguishing geographic characteristic—its flatness—is usually considered a negative. Indeed, the long stretch to the distant horizon can make you feel lonely. But the level terrain also seems to have flattened the social strata, which is far more welcoming than what you find in California's coastal communities. There are few of the super-rich here, and while Sacramento has its share of poor people, there is no great expanse of grinding poverty, no slum to speak of. Lacking hills on which the wealthy can perch and look down on the rest of town, Sacramento has neighborhoods where the well-to-do live in close proximity to the up-and-coming. The only coastal property is on the river banks, which, while lined with sprawling ranch-style mansions, are not everyone's idea of luxury living. Any sense of exclusivity is pierced by the existence of a publicly owned and accessible parkway that stretches along the American River from near the foothill town of Folsom all the way to Sacramento, where it connects with a bike trail that sits atop the east bank of the city's namesake river.

California's capital, in other words, is about as un-Californian as you can get. Its defining trait might be an almost total lack of pretense. There is plenty of puffery inside the Capitol building, of course, but ninety-nine percent of Sacramentans never go there, even though one in four in the workforce toil for one level of government or another. Get out from under the dome and this is still a very real place—even for the politicos.

Sure, the glitz is coming. The downtown is increasingly dotted with high-end restaurants, where valet parking is becoming the norm. High-rise condo towers with rents north of two thousand dollars a month are on the drawing board. And Schwarzenegger's crowd is packing the bars and bistros, giving off not just an aroma of expensive cigars but the slight whiff of a Southern California state of mind.

But so far we have taken his arrival in stride. It's not as if the city's streets are now crowded with Hummers. And those you do see tend to be spattered with mud, just back from a trip to the mountains. Around these parts, people actually drive them there.

Daniel Weintraub is the public affairs columnist for the editorial pages of *The Sacramento Bee* and his column also appears in several other California newspapers. His daily weblog, the *California Insider*, is at www.sacbee.com/insider.

Weintraub has been covering California politics and public policy for twenty years and previously worked for the *Los Angeles Times* and *Orange County Register*. During the 2003 recall campaign he was a frequent guest on CNN and Fox News and was a political analyst for MSNBC. A native of San Diego, Weintraub lives in Sacramento with his wife and two sons.

rocks in the shape of billy martin

by Deanne Stillman

I know a place in the Mojave Desert where there are rocks in the shape of Billy Martin. I visit the rocks every year to commemorate the return of spring. It makes perfect sense to me that the rocks are in the desert and not a mountain range or forest because the gone-but-not-forgotten Yankee manager was a kind of dug-out djinn, an electrical force who materialized to kick funny dust in the other guy's face and then vanished until he had to do it again.

Where did he go since we last saw him? Where all legends go—back into the desert, that big sandbox that holds America's deepest secrets. Significantly, the baseball diamond—which began on a sandlot and invokes forever—is America's most appealing attempt at taming the desert. Yet perhaps not for much longer: With consistently low television ratings for the national pastime, who knows whether it will soon be overtaken by the shifting sands?

I grew up far away from these sands, under the gray skies of Cleveland, Ohio, the place that tells you it's okay to dream, but not really. I guess that's why I always preferred the New York Yankees to the Cleveland Indians (although felt like a traitor for rooting for them until I moved to New York) and why I used to send away for cactus- es—I know you're supposed to say "cacti" but I don't like the sound of it—that you could get from places with names like Kaktus Jack's and Desert Botanicals and keep them on a window ledge near my bed. I don't know if my window ledge faced the west or not, but seeing the outlines of my little cactuses against those cloudy skies fueled my fan- tasies of the never-neverland where the turnpike went, the land where the misunderstood found understanding, the land where Zorro and Bat Masterson and Wyatt Earp wouldn't let anyone hurt you, the land where a girl named Jane lives forever as a Calamity, the land where the only thing anyone or anything really wants is a drink of water.

Much later I moved to Los Angeles, at the edge of the sands, and have lived here for the past eighteen years. In the beginning, I toiled in the television mines of Hollywood—a task not unlike haul- ing borax out of nearby Death Valley with a twenty-mule team—and found myself making frequent trips to the desert. Week after week I would flee Hollywood, the Xerox machine of America's dreams, and head for the Mojave, where they all started. I felt at home in this vast space where, if you happened to be near the right dune at the right time, you might stumble across a cosmic joke in the form of a shaman- ic workshop at the corner of Highway 111 and Bob Hope Drive, a culinary epiphany in the form of the best Hungarian restaurant this side of the Danube, a cultural oasis in the form of a biker with a used bookstore and an espresso machine, or endless miracles of nature such as the desert frogs that leap out of the sands after a rainstorm. In the Mojave, I came to understand that Los Angeles was, like my feel- ings for it, fleeting, a momentary metropolis, and I came to appreciate it as the punch line to a desert joke. Like every enclave of castles in the sand, it's overrun with fakirs. Deal-proffering bedouins named Steve wander the dunes, searching for temporary oasis. Dreams rise and fall with the caprice of studio wizards. The real thing, the elusive connection for which all who have attempted to decipher Los Angeles have yearned and failed to take into account, is the Mojave Desert, where the glitter is refracted not in the sheen of a limousine, but in flecks of obsidian and pyrite and quartz; the Mojave, where the silence is not the thunder of an unreturned phone call, but the flap of a butterfly's wings in the springtime.

The faint, ever-present L.A. pall begins to dissipate as soon as I plan to head for the desert, for the very word "Mojave" itself is comforting to say; the harmonic tones with the beginning sound of "M" or "Mo" with a soft "o" suggests mother, a safe haven, a grounding, and, in fact, the desert is female, a wide open space that is always there, waiting. And so in the time when the days begin to get longer, and there is talk of baseball, of trades and possibilities, it is to the Mojave I return. It's not difficult for me to get to the Mojave, just a one-hour drive to the north, up the 405 and over the San Gabriel Mountains, or to the east just twice as far, across the 10 (formerly route 66), through San Bernardino, and turning off at one of my favorite signs, the one marked "Other Desert Cities," just before you get to Palm Springs.

I know I am close to the Mojave when the L.A. radio stations fade from Grammy Award winners to Christian advice shows and I start receiving transmissions of other bearded evangelicals, primarily Z.Z. Top. The sun is out, my top is down, and the traffic thins. The native urge to drive fast naturally assumes command. This is fun for motorists and highway patrolmen, but not for that other Mojave denizen, the endangered desert tortoise for which I have occasionally swerved to avoid crushing as it lumbers across the pavement. Who says California has no history? I wonder, while a baby version of one of the world's oldest reptiles clambers onto the freeway shoulder and makes for some tiny blue flowers.

I cruise on and then—Oh joy! Another scenic distraction—my first Joshua tree! Now this is the true Mojave! Hi, big guy! The Joshua tree grows in only one place in the world and that is the Mojave Desert, and only at an elevation of two to six thousand feet. This misunderstood plant has taken a backseat to the towering saguaro, the Charlton Heston of cacti, the one that appears in many Westerns, sometimes wearing a sombrero, and looks like a big, welcoming, goofy person. To me, the Joshua tree is more appealing, a misfit that is the very picture of beauty and terror, a forgiving although freaky mirror that doesn't care what your name is, what you do for a living, or what kind of addiction you do or do not have. Maybe the Mormons were on to something in 1851 when they named this weird manifestation in the middle of nowhere the Joshua tree. Its shape, believed the westering followers of Brigham Young, with its uplifted and multitudinous arms, mimicked the Biblical supplicant Joshua frenetically gesticulating toward the Promised Land. Of course, they were right. But to them, the Promised Land was the future site of Salt Lake City. As far as I'm concerned, the Joshua tree is not telling people to go someplace else; it's pointing the way to other Joshua trees, whose lily petals are unfurling now to catch the morning sun. It's pointing to the rest of the Mojave, and sometimes, if you look hard through the shifting bars of light, even a coffeehouse.

Inside, a cross-section of desert locals bellies up for cheap espresso—rock climbers, handymen, end-of-the-line types who are stranded here because of DWI busts and the ensuing revocation of their drivers' licenses. I hang for a little while, but spring has sprung and I don't want to miss the fragile wildflowers that have popped open in a frenzied response to the heavy winter rains. I order a double shot in honor of Minerva Hoyt, the Pasadena socialite who in the early twentieth century lobbied for preservation of the Joshua tree, which people from Europe were uprooting and trucking out of the Mojave by the dozens, replanting them in the old country for display in botanical parks due to a cactus craze that had resulted in yet another plundering of the desert West. "L'chaim, Minerva," I say and head for Joshua Tree National Park, heading east on Highway 62, a one-way in, one-way out high-tension wire that stretches from Interstate 10 through the desert hamlets of Morongo, Twentynine Palms, and beyond. According to *Outside* Magazine, Joshua Tree National Park is home to "more weirdos per square mile" than any other national park. Read on, and be forewarned: You may count me among them, and you may be right. Once inside the park, I leave the visitor center in the dust (although not before checking the day's activity list and seeing that there are no scheduled interpretive talks, for which I always brake and swerve), anxious to see all the colors of the season and check in with my favorite cactus, which is really a member of the lily family and therefore biologically not really a cactus at all.

Deep inside this bizarre preserve, which is carpeted with the ecstatic vegetable, I park my ragtop, grab a bottle of water and hike up a trail. I pass more campers from Europe than from America, and think about this paradox: Inside the park, Joshua trees are now protected from desert-crazed Euros but outside the park, and all over the West, cacti—yes, here "cacti" sounds perfectly appropriate—are routinely blown away by gun-crazed Americans who go to the desert to shoot. But as I continue up and down a trail that is lined with paloverde and ocotillo and cholla and sage, the Mojave, as it always does, cleans my slate, and once again I am aware of only breath and blood moving through my body. The desert sand verbena is in full bloom and there is a creeping plant that looks like orange spaghetti strewn across the tops of the low-lying bushes that hug the path. In a little while, I reach my destination, a Joshua tree that is about two hundred years old and somehow makes me feel as if I were sitting in my maternal grandparents' rock garden where the daffodils and crocuses shot through the Midwestern thaw every spring, where if you got really quiet, you could hear big Rocky Colavito crunching across the sands of Lakefront Stadium as he stepped up to the plate and took the first swing of the season.

I sit down on a warm granite boulder and gaze up into the Joshua tree as the sun pulses behind. "Hey, you," it says, an alfresco support group minus the sob stories and cigarettes. "We knew you'd be back. We've been waiting. Calm down. Stop running. Tommy Hilfiger is not the heartbeat of America. I am. Bring me the arm of Fernando Valenzuela. Do you see how the gringos have stolen his stuff?" What will happen to A-Rod, I wonder, but the tree goes on. "Yes, this is what the old ballpark looked like before George Steinbrenner and Pete Rose, before cactus lamps, before all-night minimarts, before twenty-four-hour Bible theme parks, before rivers were forced to flow backwards in order to build a showcase for Kenny G. So slather on the jojoba oil and step up to the plate. We've got a fastball with your name on it. And don't worry if the game goes into extra innings. You'll have plenty of time to get home because, well, this is home . . . which is why we don't count strikes here, we don't even keep score . . . By the way, how come they got rid of ten-cent beer night?"

As the sun sets behind this cactus that's not really a cactus that grows only in the Mojave, I realize that that's the best thing about the desert: Just when you think that it explains everything, it turns around and admits that it's clueless. It takes a big piece of geography to do that; I toast the Joshua tree with my canteen and hit the road.

On my way out of the kingdom of the Joshua tree, I make my customary stop at the rocks in the shape of Billy Martin. I'm a little concerned. Has the latest swarm of earthquakes disturbed them? Apparently not; like Yankee Stadium, they haven't moved. The petrified Billy Martin is still here, gazing across the sands at the dream team, forever signaling a game-winning hit-and-run, and, as always, waiting for a drink.

Now, if you are ever out in the Mojave, the once-and-future baseball diamond, and you don't immediately come across the rocks, don't worry. Although the desert is open twenty-four hours, it has some secrets it can reveal to you only in its own time. Sooner or later you'll find them, or the rocks will find you. And if you listen closely, you may hear a distant crack of the bat, or a faint cry—"Yankee franks! Springtime! Programs!" For it's always the first day of the season out here in the sands that generate the national pastime, it's always opening day.

Deanne Stillman is the author of *Twentynine Palms: A True Story of Murder, Marines, and the Mojave*, named one of the Best Books of 2001 by the *Los Angeles Times Book Review*. She is writing *Horse Latitudes*, a narrative nonfiction history of the wild horse in the West, for Houghton Mifflin and also is working on a book about Joshua Tree National Park for the University of Arizona Press.

Stillman writes for *Rolling Stone*, the *Los Angeles Times*, *The New York Times*, *Slate* and other publications. Stillman's work is widely anthologized and her plays have been produced and won prizes in festivals around the country.

www.deannestillman.com.

how many angels

by David Kipen

People are always telling me, "I never pictured you in a pickup truck." In America, this is not a compliment. Just what kind of transportation were they picturing me in? A bookmobile?

But candy-apple red pickup trucks are good for certain things that bookmobiles are not. Helping friends move. Getting pulled over for no good reason. Feeling more rugged than you are. And, it almost goes without saying, locating the exact geometric center of Los Angeles County.

This quest will surely strike some as quixotic. For one thing, many perfectly sane individuals find the very idea of setting foot in Los Angeles County distasteful. To try positioning oneself inside it, at a point maximally remote from all its boundaries, runs counter to their fundamental urge whenever they find themselves in the region, which is to get the hell out as quickly as possible.

Also, Los Angeles has always been, famously, a city without a center. Many Angelenos will tell you that they've never visited

Downtown. They'll tell you this in the same tone of insincere apolo-
gy that intellectuals use when telling you they don't own a TV. To fill
this centerless void, city fathers in the 1960s came up with what they
called the "Centers" plan—with the accent on the 's'. (If you've ever
tried to put an accent on an 's,' perhaps while referring to the sequel
to the movie *Alien*, you'll know what an unpleasant experience this
affords both speaker and listener.) The Centers plan led to the development of pseudo-neighborhoods such as Century City and Warner
Center, but these "office parks" resembled actual, cosmopolitan centers of civic life about as much as they resembled parks. You don't hear
much about the Centers plan any more.

Yet Los Angeles has a center, if only because simple geome-
try tells us it must. For every area, there exists a point from which you
can't get any farther away from one border without getting closer to
another. In California, this point exists on a picturesque hillside just
outside the humble mountain hamlet of Coarsegold. (For a delightful
account of a journey to this centerpoint of California, I recommend
Veronique de Turenne's essay "Centered" in this very volume, though
some skepticism as to the characterization of her traveling companion
may be advisable.) In Los Angeles—the city rather than the sur-
rounding county—this centerpoint exists in the Santa Monica
Mountains beneath a tree just north of Upper Franklin Canyon
Reservoir, roughly a mile's drive from the intersection of Coldwater
Canyon Boulevard and Mulholland Drive.

We know this because a Los Angeles hiker named Allan E.
Edwards once backed a map of Los Angeles with cardboard, trimmed
away the eighty-odd neighboring municipalities, and balanced the
resulting jerrymandered, strangely bridle-like shape on the head of a
pin. There, approximately where the pin poked through the map,
Edwards tramped into the mountains and, under the bough just

described, drove into the ground a hand-chiseled silver benchmark. This benchmark remains, for my money, a work of Angeleno outsider art worthy of comparison to the Watts Towers.

But what of Los Angeles *County*, which stretches from the Antelope Valley in the north all the way to San Pedro, and from Mount Baldy to the Ventura border? If the city of Los Angeles can have a center, I asked myself, why can't the county? And if the county can have a center, my red Chevy pickup asked me, where do we find it?

According to the highly scientific map-backing, cardboard-trimming and pin-balancing method, our road lay north into the San Gabriel Mountains. Just to be sure, I had twice balanced my newly bought and trimmed Metsker Map of Los Angeles County on the point of a pushpin. This experiment had left reassuringly adjacent pinholes a short way up Big Tujunga Canyon, in what political columnist Harold Meyerson once called "the only direction in which Los Angeles refuses to grow." It's beautiful country, a lofty range of dark green mountains that divides ten million souls to the south from a few tract homes and the odd gopher to the north.

For here is the wonderful dirty secret of centerpoint-hunting: The geometric center of anything is never what or where you think it is. To be at all representative, the center of California ought to be, if not a beach, then at least a suburban backyard, or maybe an Indian casino; rather, it's a verdant, oak-dotted hillside from which the only visible sign of human visitation is the road you drove in on. The center of the City of Los Angeles ought properly to be a freeway, but instead it's a sylvan glade. And the route through the center of the Los Angeles County ought by rights to be jammed solid with commuters; come to find out, it's not even paved.

Yes, in the green shade of Mount Lukens, three and a half miles north of Sunland and an easily overshot left turn off Big Tujunga

Canyon Road, an uphill dirt track called Upper Trail Canyon Road leads straight to L.A.'s navel. Bear right at the fork, honk around the plentiful blind curves and, if you haven't landed in a ravine yet, park in the dusty clearing beside the forest service cabins. (For directions from somebody who really knows how to give directions, try hike #9 in *Trails of the Angeles: 100 Hikes in the San Gabriels*, by the late, lamented John W. Robinson.)

I notice I've lapsed into the imperative, as if anybody—besides the large black dog in my passenger seat—would willingly follow me in search of this dubious bull's-eye. But I make my living recommending books to people who'll probably never read them, so maybe giving directions to folks who'll never follow them isn't such a stretch.

By the time I've purchased our forest day-pass from the 7-Eleven on Foothill, lopsidedly jammed our provisions into a backpack and walked the few steps to the trailhead, a much bigger problem looms. I'm looking up the trail into a gently rising canyon of some kind, flanked on either side by vegetation of some kind, and it hits me: When it comes to describing natural phenomena, I'm an idiot of some kind. I was born several miles south of here on a different kind of green mountain—Vermont Avenue, where it crosses Sunset. I'm a city kid with no vocabulary, none, to articulate the splendor of what I'm seeing.

John Muir, on the other hand, in a letter to the man after whom Mount Lukens is named, once wrote of the Alleghenies that, "The forests there of oak, maple, hickory, Linden, Magnolia, Liriodendron, Oxydendron, Tupelo nyssa etc. are perfectly glorious. I'm trying to write about them." Muir's modesty is becoming, but the truth is that he's already writing about them in his letter, and doing it better than any city kid could ever hope to. He has the nature writer's perennial trump card over a citified candyass like me: Muir knows what stuff is called. I don't. Oaks, maples and magnolias, maybe I can tell apart on a good day. The others, I couldn't pick out of a lineup. Pick out of a lineup! Listen to me. Even when I'm writing about nature, my metaphors come straight out of *Hill Street Blues*.

And then I start to get angry. Easy for Muir to write well about nature. He only lived most of his life in the middle of it. Nature writers like Muir, Rick Bass, Terry Tempest Williams, Barry Lopez—they're all so self-congratulatory and smug. "Look at me, I know what an oxydendron is and you don't." Please. Like any of them could orienteer their way from downtown to the ocean if you spotted them five hours and a bus pass. Put John Muir in a left-turn pocket at rush hour and see how fast he'd beg for mercy.

But I appear to have wandered off the trail a bit. All I'm saying is, nature writing shouldn't be such a priesthood. Heaven knows plenty of travel writers parachute into cities all the time, purporting to distill the essence of a place in little more than a long weekend. Underqualified nature writers deserve only to be cut the same slack. There are no bouncers at the trailhead; the wilderness cards nobody.

Or so I told myself, as my dog and I hiked up the whatsis in the dappled shade of the doohickey. One mile, two miles, three miles, four, most of them spent fording and re-fording the twisty course of Trail Canyon Creek. We were headed for something called Tom Lucas Camp, perched near Condor Peak and something called Big Cienega. I liked the idea of Los Angeles County's center being nestled among features named after, respectively, a little-known park ranger, an endangered species and a swamp: obscurity, extinction and quicksand, all in one cleft of the map. Translate them into Latin, and it's a motto waiting to happen.

I wish I could say my compass went haywire as we approached the centerpoint. Some pebbles rolling uphill, a bobcat mating with a coyote might have been nice. The dog whined a little, but for Jake that's not exactly paranormal. We came upon a few picnic tables and a disused barbecue grill. I fed him a couple of dog biscuits, and we shared a drink. If we wanted to drive the dirt road out before nightfall, it was time to turn around.

I looked westward down the trail we'd come up on, and it had my favorite late-afternoon look: backlit by the sun, gilded, as if all the greenery had somehow come up goldenrod. Wishing I'd fashioned a benchmark of my own, something to mark the territory for whoever came after, I stretched out on the grass and fought a sense of letdown. What had I been expecting? X to mark the spot?

I felt a sharp pinprick on the nape of my neck. Great, I thought. On top of everything, a tick bite. I eased up on my elbows and investigated.

It took only a moment to find. Upright among the grass-blades, immovable as if magnetized, I swear I saw the dull tip of a steel shaft—like a pin's point might look under a microscope. Topsoil pushed up around it like a puncture. I gave the thing a tug between forefinger and thumb, only to feel the unmistakable live-wire tension of someone tugging back from below. Suddenly dizzy, I felt the whole of the county teeter and gimbal around me. How many Angelenos can balance on the head of a pin? Step gently. Only all of us.

David Kipen—Southern Californian by birth, Northern Californian by affiliation, pan-Californian at heart—is the book critic for the *San Francisco Chronicle* (www.sfgate.com/columnists/kipen/archive/).

Kipen also reviews books for Santa Monica-based KCRW, NPR's *Day to Day*, and KQED's *The California Report*.

centered

by Veronique de Turenne

We've been driving for three days. North, driving north up Highway 49 through the eastern Sierra foothills. Our destination is Downieville, a tiny town beloved by mountain bikers who swarm the hundreds of miles of vertiginous trails. Also in Downieville is the beguilingly named Sierra Shangri-la, an old-fashioned resort whose rustic cabins line the banks of the Yuba River. It's beautiful there, silent and serene, and that's where we're headed.

We've got a week to make the trip. We're celebrating my traveling companion's birthday so he gets to call the shots. Well, most of them. We left Malibu in a brand-new rental car, which is my call because the charms of David's cherished red pickup, while fine for hauling the dog or a load of firewood, exist mostly in his own mind. The truck, I'm afraid, falls far short of the needs of a road trip. In our rented sedan we've got air conditioning for the toasty ride through the Central Valley, cruise control for the numbing highway miles, and a sunroof. It's a quiet and cushy ride, which is a good thing because I'm a lousy traveler.

It's not that I don't like to travel. I do. But I like it best when it's over. I like it when the dog survived and the cats are all accounted for, when the quaint hotel wasn't awful and the collision that you're sure will make you wish you had accepted the obscenely expensive rental car insurance doesn't happen. Then I'm fine. Ecstatic, really. Hooray—what a great trip! Let's go again soon! But beforehand, in the planning stages, forget it. I hate to leave home. I hate to pack and plan and kennel the dog and get neighbors to care for the cats. I hate the day before a trip, when life as you know it grinds to a halt and the adventures that await could be good or bad or even terrific but, no matter what, must be lived in real time. Why not just stay? Turn off the phone, order in from a favorite restaurant, hike the Backbone Trail. I mean, I live in Malibu. My house stands on a bluff above the Pacific where we see whales in the winter and baby dolphins in the spring and each summer, a great horned owl raises her chicks in the chink of a rock ledge. We can hike and swim and kayak, sunbathe, stargaze and feed the hummingbirds. I don't think it's nuts to be reluctant to leave. People pay big bucks for Malibu vacations. You see them here all the time, pale as Wonder Bread on Surfrider Beach, driving real slow on Pacific Coast Highway, star-struck at Starbucks because Courtney Cox Arquette just walked by and she's even prettier in person than on TV. But eventually the plans are made and the homestead left in capable hands. And, as it always does the minute we break free of Malibu's gravitational pull, the vacation feeling kicks in. We're free. We're nomads. We're on our own, alone in the world for seven whole days. Hallelujah!

And so here we are, driving north on Highway 49, deep into California's Gold Country, into the town of Mariposa. The houses are old, gingerbready and inviting. I'm seduced. I want to rent one. I want to live here, to stop driving and become one of the locals who tell time

by courthouse bell, to be a subject of scrutiny from the clutch of eld-
erly men sitting in front of—no kidding—the general store. I want to
get a job at the Mariposa Art Gallery and sell postcards, but David has
a better idea. He's always coming up with better ideas. This time, with
the enthusiastic help of the Mariposa County librarian, David wants
to drive to the exact geographic center of California. Unlike some of
his other ideas, like buying a decommissioned bookmobile or running
for governor or the time he drove from California to New Jersey via
Canada and Mexico, this one actually makes sense. In a state this big,
where the holy trinity of Smogland, Fogland and Logland divide us,
what could the geographic center possibly look like?

And where is it? The librarian doesn't know. Well, she sort
of knows. It's back over toward the town of Coarsegold, not too far,
maybe another half hour.

Three hours later, we find it. Past Coarsegold, near North
Fork, just beyond Hensley Lake, there's a stretch of two-lane blacktop
that's sometimes called Italian Bar Road, sometimes just Road 225,
depending on the sign. Three miles down that road and suddenly, a
monument marker, a pile of rocks and a permanent survey plate
declare this place "the exact geographic center of California."

You know how when you've been driving for a while and you
finally stop the car and get out and, if you're in the country, the silence
just wallops you, brings you to your knees? That's how it is at the center of the state. You feel it, feel it on your skin and in your eardrums
and behind your eyes. Speech is too loud. The ticking of the car
engine is too loud. The sound of your own breath is too loud. In this
place, anything but the wind stirring the oak leaves, earth crumbling
as a lizard lashes his tail, grasses hissing as their stems brush together, anything but that is too loud.

It's incredible luck that this turns out to be the center of our

state. It could just as easily have been next to the deep fat fryer of a
Jack in the Box in a mini-mall in Fresno. Instead, thank God, it's here
in these rolling hills with views of an untouched valley. There are oaks
and pines, sage and wildflowers; there are vistas that give way to more
vistas until, far out on the horizon, the colors smudge and the images
blur and it's just a promise of more wilderness to come. It's California
the way we want it to be, the way we wish it still was. Anywhere you
look, anywhere you stand here in the center of the state, it's beautiful.
Sky and sun, all the shades of blue and brown, green and gold that
your soul craves. It's warm on a mid-August afternoon, warm enough
that birds call to each other but don't fly, snakes keep to the shade,
and honeybees hypnotize you with their droning monologues.

We read the marker, grateful that it's plain and workmanlike,
that it doesn't try too hard. And then we sit. Just sit and listen. No
cars. No planes. No leaf blowers. No cell phones or radios or even
other voices. Just the sounds of this place, sounds that grow louder as
we grow accustomed to it all, as it grows accustomed to us. A butterfly, a hummingbird, a beetle. I want to stay here. I want to see the sunset. I want to hear coyotes. I want to stay so long that the cuneiform
of the lizard's skin will make sense. But it's getting cold and it's getting dark and it's a long way still to Downieville, to Sierra Shangri-la.
And anyway, David's got the map open and from the look on his face,
it seems he's got another good idea.

Veronique de Turenne is a journalist and screenwriter whose work has
appeared in the Los Angeles Times, Salon, Los Angeles magazine, Variety and
many other publications.

De Turenne lives in Malibu.

returning after fire

by Chryss Yost

It's Halloween morning, 2003. For almost a week, fires have been devouring homes and charring acres of manzanita and pine along the eastern border of San Diego. We are driving through the Viejas Indian reservation, just off Highway 8 in east county. White ash is so heavy on the ground, it looks like snow. We drive past the deserted casino and outlet mall, taking a dirt road through the smoldering mountains, the back route into Descanso. After five days, the mandatory evacuation order has finally been lifted, but the main road is blocked by fire engines and California Department of Forestry buses. My brother-in-law is driving, and Mom and Stepdad are next to him in the front seat. My sister and I sit in the back. We point out anything that looks like a sign of hope—a deck that survived, a house impossibly intact in the center of a charred circle. On this familiar, unrecognizable road, we are going to find out what remains of my mother's house.

Usually, change happens slowly in the back country. People move here to slow down. In 1940, when my family first came to Descanso, there was no Interstate 8. At that time, Descanso was mostly made up of modest summer homes built for families willing to make the hour-and-a-half drive from town. In season, the small valley echoed with laughter and splashing from the community pool, the muted clop of horses' hooves down the dry riverbed and the screech of scrub jays. Now, the roads are paved with asphalt. No longer just summer homes, the houses are still sparsely scattered among the massive granite boulders. Roads curve around the ancient oak trees gently, without resistance. The soft dust kicked up by the kids and horses sparkles in the sunlight as if it were sprinkled with gold. Descanso comes from the Spanish *descansar*—to rest. In Descanso, one rests. On cold nights, each house puffs out smoke from a stone chimney.

In perhaps the only impractical choice she ever made, my Iowa-born great-grandmother bought a little cedar-shingled cabin here on an impulse. In her journal, she often asked herself why, chiding herself for the expense. With World War II in full swing, the Navy was pouring into San Diego and changing it in ways she didn't like. She wondered where the sailors and soldiers would go once the war was over.

Forty miles east of San Diego Bay, the War could be forgotten, at least for a weekend. Pictures show my great-grandmother smiling in the sunshine on the granite patio with my young grandmother and grandfather, years before my mother was born. Generations of my family grew up with a love of the soft gray-green hills, this place of peaceful refuge. In the dry hills of San Diego's Cleveland National Forest, subject to drought and Santa Ana winds, we are always aware of fire in the same way my great-grandmother was aware of the War.

Every few years, a forest fire comes too close for comfort. We watch the news closely, crossing our fingers. It has happened so often, it is almost routine. While the cabin was a weekend retreat, we never left anything there that we couldn't afford to lose in a fire, but since my mother converted it into a full-time home, the stakes have grown much higher.

It is ironic that the thing I will miss most if the house has burned down is sitting in front of the huge stone fireplace. As a child, there was no radio or TV in the cabin, and the grown-ups would play cards until late in the evening. I would read and look at the fire, closing my eyes to feel it like sunlight at the beach.

The beach has its own fires. Mission Bay, for example, always seems to smell like charcoal briquettes from barbeques and hibachis. The pallet fires always excited the imagination. In high school, my friends and I dreamed of getting a whole load of wooden shipping pallets and stacking them along the shores of Fiesta Island. We watched the pallet burners enviously, from a distance. Pallet fires could be twenty feet high, huge and roaring and primitive. The flames stretched into the darkness, reflecting on the water, transforming the people who circled the fire into the dark silhouettes of wild things. We gathered whatever firewood and scrap lumber we could find. Inspired by the orange pulse of our little bonfire, we made our teenage plans for romance and escape.

Later I fell in love with a man from Santa Barbara. Like San Diego, Santa Barbara has a history of fire. My daughter was born on the night of the Painted Cave Fire, which consumed more than four hundred homes. We thought of naming her Cassidy del Fuego—we chose Cassidy Elizabeth. Thirteen years later, scars from the Painted Cave are still visible from our house, just beyond the fire's path.

As I look out the car window now, seeing only red clay and blackened branches, I can imagine the fine lawn of green that will cover the hills in just a few months. I don't know if the house has survived, but I have learned, living with fire, that everything important rises again.

The fire surrounded Descanso on October 28, 2003, which would have been my Grandma's ninety-seventh birthday. I pray for the spirits of my ancestors to protect our little home in the hills. As we wind down the grade into the valley, I see more and more houses intact. The road is slow as it twists down toward the river road.

From across the river, we can see our cabin safe on the other side. This fire—which consumed an area as big as the city of Chicago, which razed the town of Cuyamaca and claimed two endangered species of butterflies forever—has spared our valley. Already, the scrub jays are clamoring for food.

Chryss Yost is a poet, writer and designer. She is co-editor, with Dana Gioia and Jack Hicks, of *California Poetry: From the Gold Rush to the Present* (Heyday, 2004) and, with Diane Boller and Don Selby, of *Poetry Daily: 366 Poems from the World's Most Popular Poetry Web Site* (Source Books, 2003).

A native of San Diego, Yost currently lives in Santa Barbara with her daughter.

www.chryssyost.com.

on being
a california poet

by Dana Gioia

A California poet almost inevitably feels the competing claims of language and experience. Here on the western edge of North America, we speak a European language that was transported centuries ago to a new continent. English is a northern tongue—born originally of Anglo-Saxon, Norman French and Norse. However rich its vocabulary with later overlays of Latin, Greek and Italian, this island tongue was shaped in other latitudes. By the time it had moved westward to the Pacific, Spanish was already rooted in California among the state's indigenous languages. New places and unfamiliar things had already been named, and those names have endured. This situation presents the poet with a paradox. Although English is our language, it remains at some deep level slightly foreign to our environment—like an immigrant grandparent whose words and concepts don't entirely fit the New World.

I am a Latin without a drop of British blood in my veins, but

English is my tongue. It belongs to me as much as to any member of the House of Lords. The classics of English—Shakespeare, Milton, Pope, Keats and Tennyson—are my classics. The myths and images of its literature are native to my imagination. And yet this rich literary past often stands at one remove from the experiential reality of the West. Our seasons, climate, landscape, natural life and history are alien to the worldviews of both England and New England. There were no ranches or redwoods, abalone or adobe, in the Old World or the East. Spanish—not French—colors our regional accent. The world looks and feels different in California from the way it does in Massachusetts or Manchester—not only the natural landscape but also the urban one. Our towns are named Sacramento and Santa Rosa, not Coventry or New Haven. There is no use listening for a nightingale in the scrub oaks and chaparral.

Although the seasonal imagery of British poetry—so carefully developed over centuries from close observation of nature—has both beauty and resonance to a Californian, it seems hardly less fantastic than the wizards, fairies and dragons who also inhabit those literary landscapes. To us, England is as exotic as Ilium or Cathay. Summers here are brown and dry, winters green and mild, and every month finds something blooming. The reality of California doesn't fit the poetic archetypes of the English tradition. Our history has no knights or kings, princesses or peers. We can muster a few broken conquistadors, but it was an army of indefatigable Franciscans who claimed California for their invisible, celestial empire. Wandering through a vast unarticulated landscape, they christened the rivers, mountains, harbors and settlements after Catholic saints until they had exhausted the roll call of heaven. Then they borrowed Spanish words—descriptions, nicknames and even jokes—or adapted Indian terms to complete the mission. San Pedro, Sausalito, La Mirada, El Segundo, Shasta, Cotati, Topanga and Soledad are not places one would find in Wordsworth or even Whitman. Our challenge is not only to find the right words to describe our experience but also to discover the right images, myths and characters. We describe a reality that has never been fully captured in English. Yet the earlier traditions of English help clarify what it is we might say. California poetry is our conversation between the past and present out of which we articulate ourselves.

I was born and raised in Hawthorne, California, a tough working-class town in southwest Los Angeles. Hawthorne was also my mother's hometown. Her Mestizo father had fled his reservation in New Mexico to settle on the West Coast. My father's family had immigrated from Sicily at the turn of the century and gradually made its way west. Surrounded by Italian-speaking relations, I grew up in a neighborhood populated mostly by Mexicans and Dust Bowl Okies. I attended Catholic schools at a time when Latin was still a living ritual language. I went to Junipero Serra High School, a Catholic boys' school run by the French Marianist order—many of whom were Hawaiian, Chinese or Mexican. The school was located in Gardena, which then contained the largest Japanese population in America—a city in which Buddhist temples outnumbered mainstream Protestant churches. Having experienced this extraordinary linguistic and cultural milieu, I have never given credence to Easterners who prattle about the intellectual vacuity of Southern California. My childhood was a rich mixture of European, Latino, Indian, Asian and North American culture in which everything from Hollywood to the Vatican, Buddha to the Beach Boys had its place.

My adult life has comprised equal parts of wanderlust and homesickness. The first journey, from Los Angeles to Stanford, still feels like the farthest since I was leaving the world of the working-class and immigrant family for parts unknown. Since then I have lived in Vienna, Boston, Rome, Minneapolis and New York, but I always called myself a Californian. And I always knew I would return. In 1977 my girlfriend and I went to New York, planning to stay two years. We married, had children and eventually remained there for nearly two decades. It was an exhilarating and rewarding place, but it was never truly home. In 1996 we returned to live in rural Sonoma County. It is too easy in our society for an artist to become rootless, but I believe that it is essential for some writers to maintain their regional affinities. To speak from a particular place and time is not provincialism but part of a writer's identity. It is my pleasure and my challenge to speak from California.

Dana Gioia, an award-winning poet, critic and literary anthologist, is Chairman of the National Endowment for the Arts. He is the author of *Interrogations at Noon*, *The Gods of Winter* and other volumes of poetry, as well as *Can Poetry Matter: Essays on Poetry and American Culture*. He divides his time between Sonoma County and Washington, D.C.

www.danagioia.net.

MY CALIFORNIA: Journeys by Great Writers
Edited by Donna Wares
Introduction by Pico Iyer

Cover Artwork by David Hockney
Pearblossom Hwy., 11-18th April 1986 (Second Version) 1986
Photographic Collage 71½" × 107"
© David Hockney
J. Paul Getty Museum, Los Angeles

Compilation copyright © 2004 by Angel City Press
Cover design by Kate Cohen
Interior of book designed by Amy Inouye, www.futurestudio.com

First edition
10 9 8 7 6 5 4 3
ISBN 1-883318-43-2

Chabon, Michael. "Berkeley" originally was published in *Gourmet.* © 2002 by Michael Chabon.
All rights reserved. Reprinted by arrangement with Mary Evans Inc.

Gioia, Dana. "On Being a California Poet" previously appeared in *The Misread City* (Red Hen Press).
Reprinted by permission of the author.

Haslam, Gerald. A version of "Almost Home" previously appeared in *Sierra* Magazine.
Reprinted by permission of the author.

Martínez, Rubén. "The Line" is excerpted from *Crossing Over: A Mexican Family on the Migrant Trail.*
Copyright 2001 by Rubén Martínez. Published in paperback by Picador USA in 2002, and originally in
hardcover by Metropolitan Books/Henry Holt & Co. in 2001. Reprinting by permission of Susan Bergholz
Literary Services. All rights reserved.

See, Carolyn. "Waters of Tranquility" previously appeared in *Westways* Magazine.
Reprinted by permission of the author.

Stillman, Deanne. A version of "Rocks in the Shapes of Billy Martin" previously appeared in
The Village Voice and *Newsday.* Reprinted by permission of the author.

Waldie, D.J. A version of "An Ordinary Place" previously appeared in the *Los Angeles Times.*
Reprinted by permission of the author.

Warshaw, Matt. "Surfacing," is excerpted from *Maverick's* (Chronicle Books, 2000; revised edition 2003).
Reprinted by permission of Chronicle Books.

Library of Congress Cataloging-in-Publication Data
My California : journeys by great writers / edited by Donna Wares ; introduction by Pico Iyer ;
cover artwork by David Hockney ; contributors: Mark Arax ... [et al.].-- 1st ed. p. cm.
Includes bibliographical references.
ISBN 1-883318-43-2 (pbk. : alk. paper)
1. California--Description and travel. 2. California--Biography.
I. Wares, Donna. II. Arax, Mark, 1956-

F866.2.C34277 2004
917.9404'54--dc22
2004009165

Printed in USA by Malloy Incorporated

CALIFORNIA AUTHORS.COM
WRITERS.COM

www.californiaauthors.com

ANGEL CITY PRESS

angel city press

2118 Wilshire Boulevard #880

Santa Monica, California 90403

310.395.9982

www.angelcitypress.com